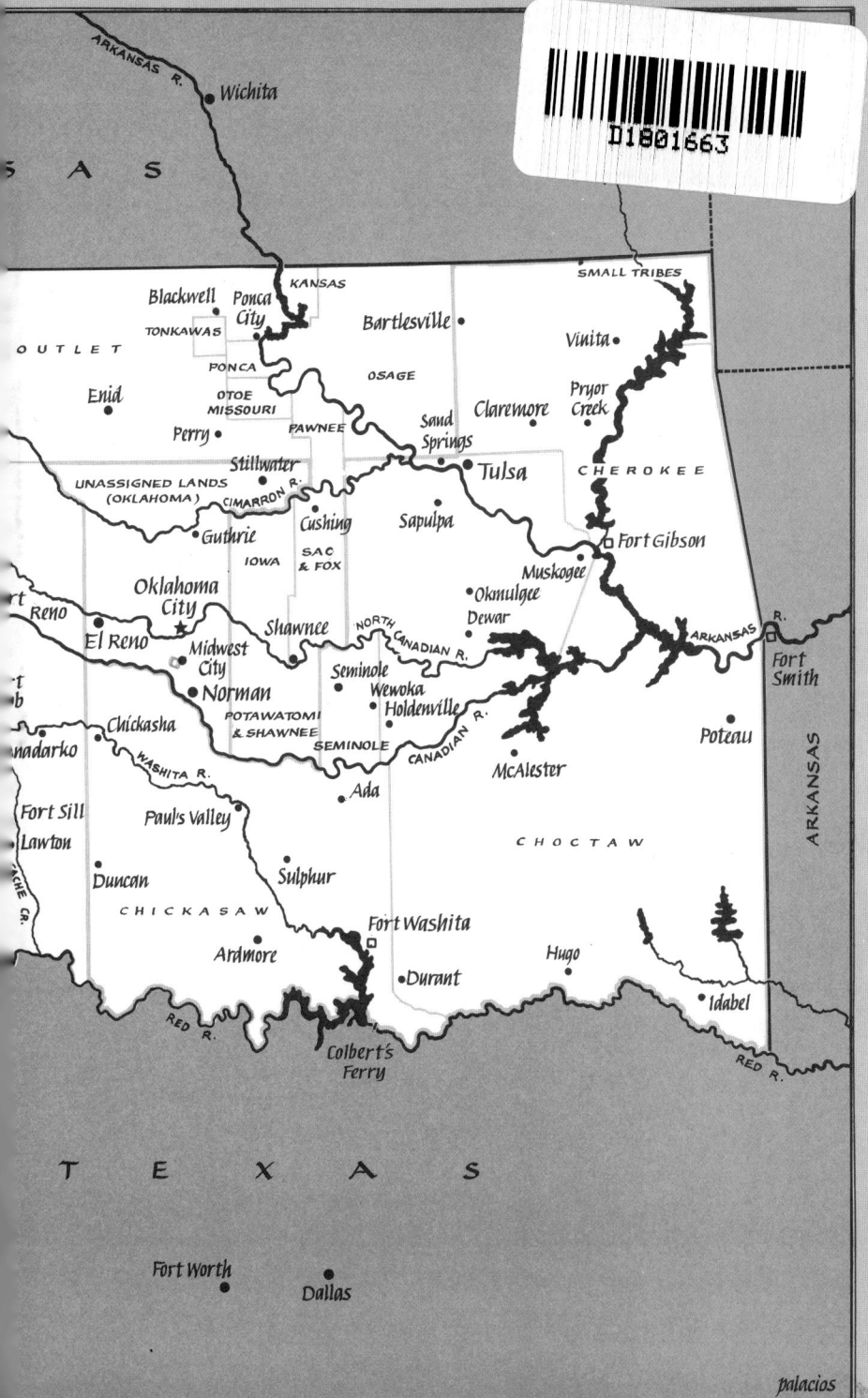

OKLAHOMA
The Forty-sixth Star

Books by Alice Marriott and Carol K. Rachlin

AMERICAN INDIAN MYTHOLOGY
AMERICAN EPIC
PEYOTE
THERE WAS ONCE A RIVER: The Fur Traders
of the Lower Mississippi
OKLAHOMA: The Forty-sixth Star

Books by Alice Marriott

THE TEN GRANDMOTHERS
MARIA, THE POTTER OF SAN ILDEFONSO
GREENER FIELDS
THE FIRST-COMERS: INDIANS OF AMERICA'S DAWN
SEQUOYAH, LEADER OF THE CHEROKEES
INDIANS ON HORSEBACK
INDIAN ANNIE
KIOWA YEARS

OKLAHOMA
The Forty-sixth Star

ALICE MARRIOTT
and CAROL K. RACHLIN

INTRODUCTION BY
ARCHIBALD C. EDWARDS

DOUBLEDAY & COMPANY, INC., GARDEN CITY, NEW YORK, 1973

Lyrics from *Oklahoma!* by Oscar Hammerstein II. Copyright © 1943 by Williamson Music, Inc. Copyright renewed. Used by permission of Williamson Music, Inc.

"Oklahoma, a Toast" by Harriet P. Camden. Reprinted by permission of Chenoweth & Green Music Company.

Poem "Oklahoma" by Mishael McMillian. Courtesy of Mr. and Mrs. Lloyd McMillian.

ISBN: 0-385-03310-9
Library of Congress Catalog Card Number 72-79408
Copyright © 1973 by Alice Marriott and Carol K. Rachlin
All Rights Reserved
Printed in the United States of America
First Edition

FOR:
Margery, the colonel's gracious lady,
who is part of Oklahoma

AND FOR:
Shirley and Gretchen,
because it is high time they visited the state

CONTENTS

INTRODUCTION   xi

PART ONE

The Land Itself, and Some of Its History

1. The Land: How It Came to Be   3
2. A Little Explanation   13
3. Magic Dogs, Wohaws, Iron Horses and Steamboats   27
4. Warpaths and Battles   45
5. Run, Run, Run for Your Living   55
6. Preparing for the Future   63
7. The Great State of Sequoyah   71
8. Fling Out the Banner—All Forty-six Stars   79
9. And Then Came Oil   87
10. The Edifice Complex   105
11. Fashions and Changes   113
12. The Buried City   123
13. Selective Cosmopolitanism   127
14. The Bad Old Days   135
15. Naughty, Naughty   139

PART TWO

The Peoples of It

16.	"Let Us Now Praise Famous Men"	151
17.	Miss Alice	169
18.	Dr. Foreman and the WPA	181
19.	Those Damn Dams	189
20.	Johnny Schmoker's Colony	193
21.	They Came and They Stayed	201
22.	What Do You Do to Get a Doctor?	211
23.	Cadillacs for Mexico	215
24.	To Wind It All Up	219
BIBLIOGRAPHY		225
INDEX		231

INTRODUCTION

The Forty-sixth Star is like someone else's notes for a lecture in a course called "My Own Life and Times" or some such thing, only these notes are those of an "A" student who has read all the assigned reading for the course and has also pinned on a few purple patches to the lecture notes to give the final flip that makes her "B+" an "A" at the final exam. No book can tell all about a state and certainly this one does not. It is not a catalogue keyed into cross lines on a highway map, not a book of reference for the historian. It is a work of art, something to awaken nostalgia and curiosity in the reader.

Neither Alice Marriott nor Carol Rachlin is a born Oklahoman. But then neither was Bill Murray nor Governor Haskell, nor Sequoyah. Nor were all the Five Civilized Tribes. This is one of the most interesting things about the state. It is new. It has progressed from an agrarian, in part nomadic, economy to an intensively industrialized one and that change has taken place within little more than the lifetime of persons still living. As interesting as the newness and the rapid maturity of the state is, the diversity—of its people, geology and topography—is distinctive.

Although the state is popularly known nowadays as an oil state, the first mineral to be exploited was coal. The topographic and geologic diversity the authors have pointed out has created a number of phenomena that are shocking to those who like to generalize about a political entity. The authors have noted how different are rainfall, climate and vegetation in the eastern part of the state from the western. The erosion of folded-and-faulted strata made for the deposits of coal in eastern Oklahoma and for oil all over. It has made for clear flowing streams on one side, and running red mud on the other, depending on whether the limestone or red beds were exposed. It also has made for the timber in the east, the cross timbers in central Oklahoma and the plains in the west. For the romantic it has made the old ford north of Highway 66 between Bridgeport and Hydro reminiscent of the crossing of the Alpheus near Olympia in Greece; and the rolling hills country from Ponca City to Pawhuska like the north of England. A young student riding through from Coalgate to Atoka on the local passenger train in the days when it still was running reports that he was utterly shocked to discover that the mother and two little girls who boarded the train at a flag stop were speaking English. He was reading Colette's *Claudine à l'École* in French. Limestone cliffs on either side of the track had carried him back to the heart of France.

Illustrating the examples of the state's diversity are the fauna and flora. The large manuals of the birds of Texas are quite serviceable in Oklahoma as are the books of wild flowers. There is no native spruce here, but in one canyon north of Anadarko there are sugar maples that are found in no other place in Oklahoma or in the country south and west of Indiana. If the inroads of the armadillo, now found as far north as Oklahoma City, are any indication, what birds and beasts of the other states not here already are at least on the way? As for the flowers that have disappeared, all those mentioned by the authors as being very rare, such as lupin, still live along the banks of Deep Fork Creek. As in all land masses far from the sea, the weather is variable. An optimum year for flowering, following an optimum year for seeding, will cover thousands of acres in the far west with gaillardia in a continuum of bright colors as far as the eye can see, or fringe a wood for miles along the highway with the bright red spikes of standing cypress, or smother a pasture with Indian paintbrush. Every year in the first weeks of May in a little patch near the town of Stigler, lovely bunches of blue delphinium bloom, and a couple of weeks later the bar ditches of Highway 40 west of Weatherford are covered with true daisies. On Highway 33 west of Watonga on the first of September the pastures are marked with the crisp and spritely blossoms of *meintzlia stricata*. It is a subtle beauty that holds the affection of people who call the forty-sixth entry to the Union home.

Informative as the background material in this work is even for the native born, the attraction is the people. The career of "Alfalfa" Bill Murray may seem, to one who did not know him when the "war" with Texas over the Red River toll bridge was trying to sizzle, a complete script for a grade-B Western. He said he would simply take away the Texans' pocketknives and chewing tobacco and they would dissolve in chagrin. By perusing these pages, every native family will remember stories just as pungent and preposterous. One family has a grandfather who came to the state as a newly admitted member of the bar back home, who in his hurry to come down and make a run for a homestead, had omitted reading the criminal section of the law. He fulfilled his solemn promise to his examiners by reading Blackstone on the train and so learned criminal law. Before his mid-twenties he was a judge of the probate court, had sent men to the insane asylum, stood on the tongue of a wagonload of lumber to marry a young couple on the road to build their home, and had even been burned in effigy by members of the Cattlemen's Convention in Fort Worth for his diligence in enforcing the laws on dipping transient herds for protection against tick fever. Up until the time of the First World War there were violent attacks on officers enforcing that law, with dynamiting of dipping vats and so on. The nieces of a very gracious lady who also came to Oklahoma as a member of the bar and who made her mark as a newspaperwoman, remember her saying that for reasons of modesty or protection she made the journey dressed in a middy blouse and wearing her hair in a long plait down her back. The conductor on the train offered her an orange and was as solicitous for her safety as though she were a motherless child of ten alone in the wicked world. Men and women, still alive, tell their children how they were brought into the world with their fathers swimming the flooded Washita to bring the doctor. He never failed his attendance at a birth if only the father would bring an extra horse that would swim the river.

The Forty-sixth Star is a provocative title because so many of the events in the book happened shortly before and not long after statehood in 1907. Although the runs for land took place west of the Cross Timbers twenty years after the Civil War, and before that time there were only cattlemen grazing their herds with the permission of the Indian tribes, and of course the missionaries to the Indians, this state was not settled by men with guns across their knees (although the plow was indeed lashed to the side of the wagon), but by farmers and businessmen and professionals who functioned as such the morning after they hit the territory.

The main history of the state is about the growth of small communities into towns and cities. Stories of the state are not of buckskin-clad Daniel Boone firing at an Indian from the shelter of his dead horse bristling with arrows. The history is about politicians matching wits with the bureaucracy of Washington. It is not the story of "a murder every afternoon at four o'clock in front of the saloons on South Broadway" but that of schoolboys dipping their folding cups into the gutters of Broadway in Oklahoma City when the breweries were forced to empty their vats, with the coming of Prohibition and statehood.

Speaking of history, no state has been more eager to preserve its glory than Oklahoma. No wedding, no christening, no inauguration nor pronouncement of the jury is official until it has been photographed. The Queen of England may have nodded in recognition of the curtsy but the presentation to the court is not finished until the handkerchief and the gloves are left in the historical society's museum. Any house whose builder has left grandchildren still holding title and of legal age is quite worthy of consideration as a historical monument. Some edifices are worthy to be preserved as monuments. It is a pity so many have been destroyed. Among those wrecked even before urban renewal came like a locust on the land in Oklahoma City was the Carnegie Library. Still standing are a Georgian clapboard house on 14th Street and St. Paul's Cathedral at 7th and Robinson, a church much sought for weddings even by unchurched people because it looks so thoroughly like a church. All three were the work of an architect named Williams. One work of George Forsyth, whose name is mentioned by the authors, should also be included here: Central High School, supposedly the most expensive and finely designed school for secondary education built in the United States in its time. The importance of architectual examples mentioned here and in the book itself is to alert any organizers of heritage areas in the state to the fact that many of the houses they are concerned about, in Oklahoma City at least, were not designed by architects and were not even the result of well-thought-out collaboration between an owner and a boss carpenter, but were merely the products of speculative builders. They are so poorly built, in many cases, that they cannot be preserved. What can be preserved and what is called to mind by Alice Marriott and Carol Rachlin is something else: the sod house. It is also the board-and-batten farmhouse, which as the farm prospered became the clapboard house—not patent drop siding. These dwellings follow a pattern as traditional as the New Mexican adobe.

The year of statehood, 1907, was a period in the history of the whole United States when the comfort and culture that a certain amount of money could buy were the same throughout the land. Latin was as well taught in Muskogee High School as it was in the Boston Latin School. A graduate of Oklahoma City High School was as welcome as a student trained at Princeton. The plays that appeared on Broadway came to the Overholser Opera House in due course, as did the concert artists and the dancers. Cripple Creek, Colorado, Denver, San Francisco, New York City, Tulsey Town (as Tulsa was still called) enjoyed the same service and more or less the same food in their best hotels. The ladies of the cities dressed in the same styles and observed the same proprieties. The men played golf in the same high-starched collars and shoes laced up to the ankle. Fort Sill and Fort Reno had polo teams that found civilian competition in the growing cities. Fort Sill and Ponca City even had hunts with English hounds and the staff in pink coats. In retrospect, the turn of the century was a pleasant era. Life was not quite so materialistic, so commercial. The '89ers always refer to the epoch as "the early days." Winston Churchill said England lost its charm and its graceful living with the war of 1914. The surviving '89ers think the forty-sixth state with its shoddy commercialism and materialism has not nearly the refinement of culture after the Second World War that it had in the early days. The descendants of those '89ers and newcomers should be grateful to Alice Marriott and Carol Rachlin for letting them know, for recalling the happier times and for indicating trails to explore. There are buildings still at Darlington. The old stockade still stands at Fort Sill. Your imagination will be stimulated by the tombstones in the Fort Reno graveyard, over bodies of the unknown dead found on the prairie, and the body of a post commander who loved the place and bodies of German prisoners of war of World War I. You will be amazed at the size of the hackberry tree coming up through the foundation of the hospital building at Fort Towson and the beautiful brickwork in the vaulting of the magazine there. Drive from Oklahoma City to Chandler, over the Hogback, with a detour through Spencer to see little Natchez-on-the-Deep-Fork. It takes a loving eye and an imaginative feeling for history to see Natchez in Spencer. It's worth a try.

In Oklahoma, some people still alive today began their schooling in foreign-language schools. The most common language seems to have been German, probably because so many Germans settled in Oklahoma. Some Oklahomans born during territorial days still can be surprised when they travel an unfamiliar road by discovering a church school or mission perched prominently on a hill or tucked away in a little valley. In the McAlester area there are Italian and Welsh settlements with vestiges of the culture still noticeable, and the Italians seem to have kept to their cooking much better than the Germans. Czech settlements at Prague and at Yukon still preserve native cooking and dress in native costumes at festivals now being revived as part of the identity crisis that is used to explain everything from the hippies to the hot rod motor car and the prevalence of the cowboy boot. There is many a wearer of that footgear who couldn't stay on a wooden horse on a merry-go-round and has to explain the rationale of his costume by saying the high heel is wonderful for relaxing the foot on the accelerator of a truck or sports car. An inspection of the Czech festivals shows a sincere effort to maintain the ethnic cultural patterns. Two or three hours spent at one of them in Yukon in 1971 revealed a pattern of gaiety unknown in the cosmopolitan centers such as Oklahoma City and Tulsa. Old gentlemen with white hair were dancing with tall blond girls in a roped-off section of the street. The town was full of young girls in Czech dress, tending shops and apparently changing places every hour or so with the dancers. A huge tent covered crowds milling about booths where sandwiches and sausages and cakes were for sale. A discreet inquiry brought the information that an establishment reached through a doorway painted to resemble an Old World village inn served beer, but the informant had never been there. It was perhaps an indication of his character rather than a reflection on it that the jollification that went on in the bar was sustained entirely on 3.2 beer, the only kind obtainable in Oklahoma.

Until recently, St. Gregory's Abbey of Benedictines at Shawnee had brothers who spoke Basque, as did the founders. The abbot oversees and acts as spiritual father to three parishes in California, whose communicants came from the Basque Provinces of Spain to herd sheep. *The Forty-sixth Star* lights all the world, in its way.

ARCHIBALD C. EDWARDS

OKLAHOMA

I give you a land of sun and showers,
And summer the whole year long.
I give you a land where the golden hours
Roll by to the mocking birds' song.
Where the corn grows high
'Neath the smiling sky,
And the quail whistles low in the grass,
And fruit trees green bear a burden sweet,
To perfume the winds that pass—
    Oklahoma, Oklahoma, fairest daughter of the west,
    Oklahoma, Oklahoma, 'tis the land I love the best,
    We have often sung her praises,
    But we have not told the half,
    So I give you, Oklahoma,
    A toast we all can quaff.

Verses by Harriet Parker Camden
(The first state song)

OKLAHOMA!

Oklahoma! Where the wind comes sweeping o'er the plains!
And the waving wheat can sure smell sweet,
When the winds come right behind the rains.
Oklahoma! Every night my honey lamb and I
Sit alone and talk,
And watch the hawk,
Making lazy circles in the sky.
We know we belong to the land,
And the land we belong to is grand.
And so we say, Ay-yippee-yippee-ay!
You're doing fine, Oklahoma,
Oklahoma! O-K-L-A-H-O-M-A! Oklahoma! OK!

Verses by Oscar Hammerstein II
(The second state song)

PART ONE

The Land Itself, and Some of Its History

CHAPTER 1

THE LAND: HOW IT CAME TO BE

In the beginning, there should have been two stars; the forty-sixth and the forty-seventh. Oklahoma is not just one state. It is split plumb spang in two down the middle, as some of its citizens say, by a belt of woodland, running north and south, which divides it into eastern and western domains. The central part is, and has always been, a kind of no man's land.

The belt—the Cross Timbers—follows the course of the Permian red beds and runs from the Gulf Coast of Texas to the Ozark uplands in Missouri. It is either poor, thin, red soil or bare sandstone which is gradually eroding into sand. The sandstone was first laid down by shallow lakes 230 million years ago over the oil-bearing sands and shales of the earlier Devonian formations. The only valid reason anyone is ever interested in the Cross Timbers is the black stealthy sticky wealth that lies beneath them.

On the east side of the Timbers the earth is more recent, laid down principally by water erosion during the latest of the Pleistocene periods, about the time that human beings first began to cross the land bridge between Asia and North America. The eastern part of Oklahoma is fertile river bottoms, separated by limestone hills. One of the rivers—the Glover River—may well be the last free-running unpolluted river in the United States. Besides the fertility of the river bottoms, eastern Oklahoma uplands are well wooded and a rich source of standing timber. In time, commercial lumbering operations and devastating forest fires will have destroyed most of the original virgin timber, and few of the replacement stands have yet matured. At this writing, Glover River and its pine forest drainage area are being threatened by commercial lumbering, as well as by arsonists. Conservationists may save this one untouched piece of woodland. They may.

West of the Cross Timbers the short-grass plains begin, still laid out in the land forms of the ocean bottom they once were. About the time that the Permian sands were laid down an earthquake caused an upheaval in southwestern Oklahoma, and the Arbuckle and Wichita mountains resulted in the form of islands. They have eroded now, only the granite cores of the Wichitas and the Arbuckles' vertical fossil-rich strata show on the surface, but both small ranges, which are hardly even hills when compared to the Rockies, are geologists' paradises.

To speak of western Oklahoma as plains country, as one usually does, is to invite comparison with Kansas and the other northern Middle Western states. But the short-grass country of the Texas panhandle, of all western Oklahoma, and of a small portion of southwestern Kansas is not flat prairie. It still rolls with the steadiness of waves on water.

Here, too, the soil is thin and poor; here, too, it overlies oil-bearing sands and shales. Since the early 1900s, men have been trying to alter the land forms of western Oklahoma;

to plow and plant them with cotton, or with wheat and small-grain forage crops. Again and again the short-grass country has defeated men's efforts. Plow its slopes up and down, in the old-fashioned way, or plow them following their contours, as is now done, it makes no difference. Flash floods pour across the face of the land in any direction, laying fields bare and gashing new gullies through them.

The short-grass country is not land to sit down meekly and take what comes. In eastern Oklahoma, the limestone soils submit to being denuded and plowed over. Not so in the west. Here, if all else fails, nature can send a tornado or a blue norther—the latter one of those killing storms before which cattle and men drift helplessly, to huddle, frozen and starved, in the corners of the fences that are inevitable to a white man's world.

Only in the north-central part of the state, where the Timbers bend eastward toward the Ozarks, is there land rich in oil as well as food potential. Here the native bluestem, unlike the grama grasses of the lands west of them, grow "belly-deep to a man on a horse," and men boast that their fathers' pastures, on which cattle thrive, have never been plowed or planted to any grass but bluestem, which seeds itself.

And the Cross Timbers? So what, the Cross Timbers? They are a geographical dividing line, and they are also a cultural demarcation. It was a habit of early explorers of the region to dismiss them as "impassable." Coronado turned back from their western boundary, and De Soto, also exploring for Spain in 1540, turned back from the eastern edge of the Timbers for the same reason: armed and mounted men could not penetrate that belt of woodland.

The trees of the Cross Timbers are blackjack, pin oak, post oak, hackberry, elm and cottonwood in the main, with an occasional soil-consuming native cedar scattered here and there. All these trees are resilient to an ax blade and all are perfectly useless except for firewood. The trees are lashed and bound together by bush honeysuckle, briars, wild grapevines, blackberries and buckbrush. One of the writers of this book spent some formative years on an acreage in the Cross Timbers east of Oklahoma City. She is here to testify that what a twelve-year-old armed with a Boy Scout hatchet can't get through may safely be termed impassable.

Rivers run—in a manner of speaking—through the Cross Timbers. They head in the highlands of the Oklahoma Panhandle, where the country reaches a height of a mile on its way up to the Rockies, and trickle across the state to the swamps of the southeast, where the elevation is barely six hundred feet above sea level.

These rivers start as flash flood streams and retain much of that character; either flooding the land on either side of their sandy beds before they spread out into bayous and sloughs, or withdrawing entirely in the dry season, to leave their beds treacherous quicksands. The rivers that rise in the west never have the sweet steady flow of the eastern Oklahoma rivers that rise in the north and course, by way of the Mississippi and its tributaries, to the Gulf of Mexico.

Nominally, the Red River divides Oklahoma from Texas. It is a flooding, quicksandy stream, larger than the rivers north of it in central Oklahoma. Its course should have been passable for canoe navigation even before European exploration began, but that was not the case. Upstream from its confluence with the Arkansas, from which the joined streams flow into the Mississippi, the Red River was blocked by "the Great Raft." This was a packed mass of driftwood, washed down from smaller tributaries and from the upper reaches of the Red River itself. The raft was packed so dense and solid that a man could walk across it dry-footed.

The Arkansas, which rises in the Colorado foothills and flows across central Kansas into eastern Oklahoma, joined the Red below the raft. In one way or another, the Arkansas has always been a navigable river, while the Red was not.

In fact, there have been many times when it was impossible to determine exactly where the bed of the Red River was; if it were in Oklahoma or Texas, or neatly running a steady course to divide the two states down its center line. Legislation was finally required to solve the problem. The south bank of the Red is in Texas. The north is in Oklahoma and the river is on its own.

Land, and the people who live on it, shape each other. Eastern Oklahoma is traditionally southern. Cotton culture, slavery, fox hounds, and restrained elegance all were in Muskogee, Tahlequah, Fort Gibson, and Okmulgee in diluted forms, and the speech that would hallow them still lingers on some tongues, but these are thin imitations at best of the true culture of the old Southeast.

The Miami-Pitcher area of extreme northeastern Oklahoma was to become a dumping ground for Indians from all over the United States, as their lands were ceded or expropriated. It was a stony, hilly land, cut by such major rivers as the Illinois, the Verdigris and the Grand. No one could guess that below the shallow soil, on which little would grow, were wealths of minerals: zinc, lead, pottery clay and even fine sand for glassmaking.

It was no man's land in the beginning; where the Cross Timbers yielded to the prairies and anyone could hunt. This is the land Washington Irving described on his way from St. Louis to Fort Gibson as "arid, barren and inhospitable country." It was the land where Pierre Chouteau led his band of displaced Osages and a few Otos, and where they traded for buffalo hides with the western tribes. Nobody wanted it, and remnant tribes could be settled there. No one foresaw what cities were to develop there, north of the Three Forks, Pitcher and Miami, of course; Vinita, Afton and Delaware. Mining of coal and zinc and the pumping of oil brought richness to the area.

Western Oklahoma was buffalo country to begin with and is cattle country today. No amount of coaxing, cajoling, fertilizing, ripping apart the land or planting trees not native to the area to serve as windbreaks will ever make western Oklahoma anything but grazing land. Only the short native grasses can hold the soil in place before the blasts of wind that create blowouts in Nebraska's sand hills and dust bowls in what was once known as "the Great American Desert."

In January of 1971 it was estimated by the American Cattlemen's Association that the fat cattle and slaughtering capital of the United States had moved itself to Guymon, in the Oklahoma Panhandle, and the stockyards of Chicago, Kansas City and St. Louis were being abandoned. Only Omaha was left to compete with Guymon.

The land rules man. If you can't lick it, jine it. What feeds and maintains buffalo will also feed and maintain Angus, Hereford, Charolais and Durham cattle. Not dairy stock, but good solid blocky producers of the "well-marbled firm red beef" of which butchers boast and which breeders are always seeking new and improved ways to inseminate artificially. Such livestock has now reached the point of confirmation where reproduction by natural methods cannot be accomplished.

And again, what about the Cross Timbers? Here, in the

center of the state, began the true written history of Oklahoma as Oklahoma, for here is the no man's land that government surveyors lost for a couple of centuries; the land that was missing even from the official maps that were drawn after the Louisiana Purchase. It was to the Cross Timbers and the country bordering them on the west that David Payne, a clerk in the Department of the Interior, led his band of Boomers across the Kansas line and began taking up individual tracts for homesteading. This was where men first began to stake their claims to quarter sections; to assert their right to hold and clear one one-hundred-sixty-acre plot, or quarter section. This is one quarter of the six hundred forty acres that make up a square mile. From the time the stakes are driven in, the claimant is free to stand in the middle of the area they enclose and with rifle, shotgun or cannon, if one is available, drive off intruders and counterclaimants. The land is *his*.

Federal regulations governing land claims and claimants require that certain improvements—houses, barns, fences, etc.—be constructed on the land within a designated period of time, and that the improvements be maintained for a further period if the claimant is to assert his right to his homestead and claim legal title to it indefinitely. Homestead land may later be cut up, subdivided, sold, engulfed in a city, or even flooded by construction of dams and waterways, but it still remains homestead land, and as such is exempt from land taxes. Improvement taxes for schools, paving, water and sewage systems, etc., however, may be levied against it.

Oklahoma is by no means the only state where homestead lands could or can be claimed and held, but it is the only state where three fourths of the land area was occupied by claimants in a succession of land openings.

Only in parts of western Oklahoma do the original occupants of the land—the Comanche, the Kiowa, the Plains Apache groups, the Cheyenne and the Arapaho—still linger. Ironically, their holdings are restricted to the same individual quarter sections as those belonging to their white neighbors. These allotted lands, assigned to individual Indians before statehood in 1907, cannot be land-taxed, and only under unusual conditions can they be sold. Allotted lands occupy about one third of western Oklahoma.

Large portions of the Mississippi Valley were opened to veterans' claims after the Civil War, and it was then that the hundred and sixty limit was established. Much of Missouri, Ohio, Indiana and Illinois were settled in this way. Smaller parcels of homestead land can still be claimed in parts of Colorado, Utah, Arizona, California and Alaska. True, by the 1970s, the land available for homesteading has been whittled down to the land nobody else wants, far from water, on steep mountain slopes or covered with immovable rocks, but there *is* still homestead land to be claimed in the United States. Amos Hopkins-Dukes, a Kiowa, has for years spearheaded a movement to claim these lands for Indians, and settle the people far away from the treaty-restricted allotment and reservation areas in other states.

To stake a claim anywhere takes vision and courage. It means uprooting oneself from familiar surroundings, if one is accustomed to a settled life, or for the footloose and fancy free, tying oneself forever to the same quarter of a square mile. As much determination and foresight is needed for one as for the other. Not every cowboy wanted to stay in one place, not even after "bob-wire played hell with Texas" in the 1870s, when the ranges were fenced forever. If a man accepted the responsibility of staying put and developing his acreage he lost his freedom and much of his status in his own eyes. A man afoot, he was no man at all.

Other claimants, the dispossessed of eastern industrial cities, immigrants from over the seas, or the tenant farmers of the war-ravaged South, saw in land claims hope and the promise of a status they had never had. To them, staking a claim was not a sacrifice of social standing but a means of acquiring status as landowners. Any other sacrifice was worth the ownership of land.

For the phrase "to stake a claim" has many more connotations than land ownership. A man stakes his claim to a girl when he puts an engagement ring on her finger, and secures his title when he adds a wedding band to it. A woman stakes her claim to her house when she hangs curtains—even curtains made of flour sacks—over her windows and covers her floor with homemade braided rugs. The arrival of the cooking stove and a storage cupboard for food secures her title to even a mean and temporary shack.

A politician stakes his claim to a public office when he has outvoted or bought off his opponents and takes title when he is sworn in. An office worker stakes his claim to a job when he sits down at a desk and takes title with his first pay check. In homestead country, the phrase has never been forgotten. It is still in daily use and probably will continue to be.

To hold a claim, in whatever form long enough to secure title, takes guts. That strange combination of courage, determination, wry humor, physical stamina and compassion, combined with opportune forgetfulness, is a peculiarly American quality. Perhaps it reached its highest point of development in Oklahoma's Will Rogers (he was born here, and we claim him, although now he belongs to the world).

Oklahomans are still near enough to the frontier to be both

proud and ashamed of it. Three of the four states that have been admitted to the Union since the forty-sixth star was hung have longer written histories, more intellectual and social distinction in the public eye, and went through their growing pains long before Oklahoma came to be. Only Alaskans can really understand Oklahomans. Only they, besides Oklahomans, know what it is to stake a claim—and HOLD IT.

CHAPTER 2

A LITTLE EXPLANATION

This is a very personal book for both its writers. One came to Oklahoma at the age of seven with her family. The state was only three years older than she was. The other came alone, after Oklahoma had celebrated its semicentennial anniversary, as an adult and of her own free will and accord, to learn some things about American Indian life that she could learn nowhere else.

That means, of course, that our personal experiences will be reflected in our telling of Oklahoma's story, and that our two radically different points of view will have to be reconciled if possible. If the book falls between two stools that will be natural, right and inevitable. Only remember that both writers equally are introduced from the lecture platform as "Not *quite* Oklahomans," for they were born in other places.

Outside the state, two facts about Oklahoma are well established in the public mind. These are that the place has oil wells and it has oil-rich Indians.

Well, Oklahoma has many oil wells and the refineries and

processing plants that go with them, it is true. The oil industry ranks fourth in the state's economy. After wheat, cattle raising, boating and boat manufacturing comes oil.

There are a few rich Indians in each of the state's fifty-seven tribes, but not all of them are oil rich. Some grew rich by inheritance of allotted lands. Others made it on their own, in the professions or in business. But the vast majority of Oklahoma's Indians belong to middle-to-low-income families, and some of them exist from hand to mouth.

We have played hopscotch in this book with geography and chronology. So much went on at once, in so many places considerably distant from each other, that only the most disorderly sort of order is possible in telling about them.

Some of these stories have come to us from participants or their descendants. Some are regional legends only vaguely founded on fact. Yet others derive from a kind of gossipy folklore endemic in families, and in still others we have actively participated ourselves. Some can be found in other books or in library archives, and their sources can be checked. Others can not. Whatever their sources, these stories of Oklahoma and Oklahomans are as true as red dust or the pounding hoofs of horses; as true as a straight-fired Springfield .45/70 rifle or a war whoop or the blare of a cavalry trumpet.

Oklahomans are hybrids and always have been, and they are proud of the fact. The state is situated one third nearer the Mexican than the Canadian border, and is equidistant from New York and Los Angeles. Oklahoma is in the same latitude as Morocco, Afghanistan and Central China. Like the peoples of those other lands, Oklahomans are by turns arrogant, shy, unpredictable and uproarious. If the United States is the melting pot of the world, Oklahoma is the melting pot of the United States.

It is a truism of show business that if you want to make people laugh, you identify yourself or your plot with a place name that has a "k" in it. One thinks immediately of Kankakee, Kokomo, Oshkosh b'gosh—and Oklahoma. There is something endearingly risible about the sound, and many comedians and writers have capitalized on it.

Oklahoma first burst on the world as a place in its own right when the Rodgers and Hammerstein musical *Oklahoma!* opened on Broadway in 1943. On the first anniversary of its opening, the late Mr. Fred Jones, an Oklahoma City Ford dealer, and Mrs. Jones presented the Broadway cast with a birthday cake. Twenty-six years later, in 1969, the Surrey Singers (and guess where they got *that* name) of Oklahoma City University presented Mr. and Mrs. Jones on their wedding anniversary, which was also the anniversary of the first show's opening, with a new production of the musical—and a large cake.

Granted that the sounds and words of genius do endure, still this was a survival record for most musicals. *Oklahoma!* has never been cheapened, never suffered from overquaintness, and has always been as easy or as difficult to produce as any cast wanted it to be. The word "Oklahoma" will always provoke warmth and smiles, even from people who have never seen the place.

Lynn Riggs's *Green Grow the Lilacs* had captured the pain and dignity of pioneer life in Oklahoma before his "folk opera," studded with folk songs, had been transmuted into a long-term New York happening. Riggs, a Cherokee Indian by descent, knew the people and their lives, and he wrote from the inside out. The later composer-lyricist team did not know Oklahoma firsthand as a place, and they were certainly not familiar with the local vocabulary, customs, flora or fauna, and what Riggs had tried to show the world. Because of them the name of an obscure southern Middle Western state passed into the national vocabulary. It would almost seem that there is nothing to be added to their accomplishment.

There is more and much more. Our aim in the pages that follow is similar to Professor McGuffey's in his *Electic Fifth Reader*, on which all Oklahomans over fifty, native or not, cut their literary teeth, to "educate, elevate, and entertain."

The Five Civilized Tribes, the Cherokee, Chickasaw, Choctaw, Creek and Seminole, had been called "civilized" by the English colonists of the south Atlantic seaboard, because their social structure resembled that of the English. There was a principal chief, or "king" as the English designated him, a House of Chiefs, older more experienced men, and a House of Warriors, who were what the name implies. Together they formed a bicameral body which consulted with and was consulted by the principal chief.

These tribes lived in walled and stockaded towns, wore elaborate ornaments, had priests and temples and were agriculturalists. The members of the Five Civilized Tribes early began intermarriage with the English and, later, with the French, and it is doubtful if there was a full blood in any of these tribes after 1850.

After the War of 1812, it became clear to the Cherokees, particularly, that their lands in Georgia and the Carolinas were being rapidly settled by squatters' rights by the citizens of the new United States. The "Old Settlers," as they called themselves, moved westward and settled on lands formerly belonging to the Osage and Quapaw, between the White and St. Francis rivers in Arkansas Territory.

In 1827, another Cherokee group, led by John Rogers, a

powerful rival of the then Principal Chief John Ross, settled at the Three Forks where the Arkansas, Verdigris and Illinois rivers joined, near the present town of Fort Gibson, Oklahoma.

In 1829, Rogers' adopted son, Sam Houston, left the governorship of Tennessee and came out to join the Cherokees. Within about a year he married Rogers' daughter, Diana, or Talihina. His influence with Rogers' group and with the Old Settlers was strong.

Houston repeatedly urged the Cherokees to go south with him, into Texas, which was then a part of Mexico. After Diana's death, in 1833, he went at the head of a small band of Cherokees. The Indians, however, found the Texicans, or Texas-Mexicans of Anglo descent, even less hospitable than the people who had surrounded their former homes, and they returned to the United States.

Houston himself remained in Texas, to become the first President of the Texas Republic and later first Governor of the state of Texas. He often spoke with deep affection of "his people," the Cherokees, but he never returned to them.

The first occupants of Oklahoma proper were the southern Siouans: Osage, Quapaw and Ponca, and the Caddoan-speaking Wichita. These tribes were settled along the Arkansas and its tributaries at the time La Salle descended the Mississippi in 1675. As the Cherokees infiltrated Arkansas and went west to the Three Forks, these tribes were pushed aside. From 1804 to 1838, the movement can be mapped, a steady one hundred miles westward every ten years.

Rogers had headed the removal faction. John Ross, elected Principal Chief of the Cherokees, opposed removal and insisted that the Cherokees remain on their old lands. Andrew Jackson, who may not have coined the phrase that "the only good Indian is a dead one," certainly acted on that principle. Prodded by politicians and southern white plantation owners, and needing little prodding to begin with, Jackson began the push for removal of all the Civilized Tribes. The Georgia State Militia took an active part in "cleaning out the woods," and often Indians were driven from their homes without time to gather together even a few simple necessities. The whites moved into Indian farmsteads and plantations and took over.

One story of the period is told that a woman was feeding her chickens when the militia stopped at the farmyard gate. She threw the corn to the chickens and ran through her house, sweeping up clothing and bedding before she rushed to the upper fields where her husband and sons were working, to warn them. By the time they returned to the house, it was in flames and the chickens, with their heads wrung off, were flapping around the farmyard.

And then there was Tsali, the immortal hero of the Cherokees. He, his wife, their sons and daughters-in-law defied removal and escaped into the woods, where they were finally run down by the troopers. As men who attempted to escape, Tsali and his sons were sentenced to be shot out of hand. Amanda, Tsali's wife, chose to die as she had lived since girlhood, with her husband. The other women had small children, and chose to live and care for them.

Then Tsali spoke one of the most touching short orations in American history. "A man has one life to live," he said. "He plants his seed, and if he has good fortune and good crops, as I have had, it ripens. My older sons, too, have had their chance to live on in others. But this, my youngest, is fourteen only. He has had no chance to plant his seed. Let him go free. Give him his chance." Behind them, as the youngster and his sisters-in-law turned away, tied together by the troopers' ropes, they heard the shots that told the end of the rest of the family.

From uplands, from lowlands and from the valleys between the hills, the Indians were herded together in concentration camps along the Tennessee, Hiwassee, Tombigbee and other rivers to wait for transportation to the nations west. Thousands died of disease and filth and hunger. Finally they were transported overland and on keel boats on the rivers to what was to become Indian Territory—the woods and hills of eastern Oklahoma. Of the Cherokees, the only tribe on whom we have anything approaching statistics kept by the United States troops that removed them, only one tenth survived the journey.

None of this was done without legal justification, of course. The new United States followed the English colonial policy of "divide and conquer." The Rogers family, with their relatives the Ridges and the Boudinots, were persuaded to sign "treaties" with the United States, ceding their eastern lands in exchange for those in the west. Ross and his faction strongly resisted not only removal but the signing of any such treaties. To this day the Rogers-Ross feud persists, and though members of each family have married into the other, the political difficulties have never been resolved. It cannot truly be said that there is or ever has been a Cherokee "tribe," and the same is true of the Creek, Choctaw and Seminole.

After removal the rich remained rich and aristocratic; they had been of the upper class before the white invasion. The poor remained dirt farmers. Both groups were industrious and intelligent. The upper classes acquired Negro slaves almost as soon as their non-Indian neighbors did. The Civilized Tribes had consolidated into four main bodies before the Revolutionary period: the Iroquoian-speaking Cherokee in the north, with the Muskhogean-speaking units of the Creek Confederacy south of them, and, farthest south of all, the Chickasaw and Choctaw, who were also Muskhogean-speaking.

The upper classes in all these tribes sent their sons north to the new universities that were springing up in New England and northern New York and Pennsylvania. The same families imported English governesses and tutors for their younger children and their daughters. The stockades that had once surrounded their towns, and the temples around which the towns had been built, had disappeared, but the town communities remained, and often retained their former names such as Tulsa, Okmulgee and Tahlequah. In the new towns council houses and the town houses of the members of the bicameral legislatures were built near mission churches and schools.

Each tribal council had a Principal Chief, a House of Kings (the senior body), and a junior House of Warriors, from Cherokee New Echota in North Carolina to Choctaw Nuniwaya, far to the south in Mississippi.

The tribal councils sent their own representatives to the courts of Versailles and St. James, where the ambassadors were well received. Some of the ambassadors married abroad and remained in their wives' countries; others brought their European wives home with them. Fox hunting was fashionable, for, except among the Choctaw and Chickasaw, where French contacts were strongest, the dominant European influence was English. Many Choctaw and Chickasaw carry French names to this day, although the principal chiefs of the Creeks have carried the Scots name McIntosh for many terms, and the Rosses and the Rogerses were always the leading families among the Cherokees.

A fifth Civilized Tribe, the Seminole, came into being after the Revolution. They were the resistance, made up of Mikasuki, Creek, Hitchiti, Natchez, and the few remaining Mobilians and Biloxi. They gave refuge to escaped Negro slaves, and their Muskhogean name for themselves, Samano, translated into English, means Runaways. At the head of Lake Okeechobee and deep in the Florida Everglades they built their towns, held their dances and council meetings and carried on their old religious rituals into the twentieth century. Those who were more "progressive," and more closely allied to the Creeks proper, were included as a fifth civilized tribe in the westward removal.

Each of the removed tribes set up a new national capital, which was in time to become a county seat. There was Tahlequah of the Cherokees in the north, Okmulgee of the Creeks in the center of eastern Oklahoma, Wewoka of the Seminoles south and east of Okmulgee, Tuskahoma of the Choctaws and Tishomingo of the Chickasaws south and west of the Seminole. In each a national capital building was constructed of brick or native stone, and all are still standing except the Seminole capital. The Creek Council House at Okmulgee has become a local museum, while the others, of which Tahlequah is the best preserved and is in present use as the Cherokee County court house, are used for tribal gatherings of many kinds.

John Ross, the principal chief of the Cherokees at the time of the removal, took up land at Park Hill, south of Tahlequah. On the grounds at Park Hill, "seminaries" for young men and women were built by the Moravian missionaries with tribal funds. These were the first college-level institutions constructed west of the Mississippi. The Cherokee National Press was established in the basement of the Council House at Tahlequah, and began issuing a bilingual monthly newspaper, *The Cherokee Phoenix*. The other four tribes did not have their own presses, but had their codified laws, the Bible, some hymn books and some school texts printed in English fonts by job printers, first in the East and then in their own communities.

Oak trees grow abundantly in eastern Oklahoma and bear large acorns. Swine thrived on the acorns, and Oklahoma hams and bacon became famous as did the dried plums, grapes, wild fruits and berries, apples, pears, peaches and apricots that the women prepared. The last four fruits were not native, but were European importations to the eastern states. Root stocks had been carried west by thrifty Indian housewives.

Everything that a family did not actually need for its own subsistence in the years immediately following the removal went into trade with other tribes or with the white settlers who were nestling unobtrusively into the Indian country. Iron pots and kettles, too heavy to carry on the long journeys overland, had been left behind, and dim memories of grandmothers who made their own pottery for cooking and eating had led women to make crude pottery and to revive the art of fine basketmaking, which they had never really lost. This was what anthropologists call "secondary primitivity." Gourds had replaced metal spoons and dippers for a time, and then trade brought back the metal utensils, and the gourds were almost forgotten.

In only one matter were eastern Indian women adamantly opposed to change in kitchen equipment. Even after waterpowered stone gristmills were established and on into 1973, when one built in 1840 is still in operation, many women preferred to pound their own corn meal in mortars made of burned-out tree trunks, using pestles of wood, one end sharpened to fit the hole in the log, the other a massive ball to be lifted and add its weight to the pounding. The chaff was winnowed from the meal in flat, three-sided open baskets, from which the pounded grain could be tossed in the air so the chaff could blow away.

The eastern tribes had been more or less loose confederacies and bands before removal. The western journey had created the "tribes" as we know them today, even if it had not entirely done away with factionalism, or with a sharp consciousness of the differences in wealth and status between the "full bloods" and the "mixed bloods."

"If you had to choose between a McIntosh or a Deer in appointing a principal chief for the Creeks," a commissioner of Indian Affairs once asked us, "which would be your choice?"

Our immediate impulse was to suggest abandonment of the custom of presidential appointment of principal chiefs through the Bureau of Indian Affairs, which had begun after the Civil War, and let the Creeks cast their own votes. Diplomatically, the only possible answer that could be returned was that while the nearly full-blood Deer family undoubtedly came closer to representing more Creeks than the mixed-blood but shrewd McIntoshes, it was the McIntosh family which had repeatedly demonstrated the skill which was required for dealing with non-Indians, so a McIntosh was suggested and duly appointed.

A few years later that same principal chief attended a reunion of the McIntosh clan of Scotland in Edinburgh, flaunting a feathered Cheyenne war bonnet (the Creeks never wore war bonnets) above his kilt and sporran. He returned to start a weaving industry among the Creeks, and designed "clan tartans" for the Deers, the Cranes and the Tigers, among others. Charley had gone over the waters—and returned triumphant!

Only the Chickasaw had not traveled westward in sorrow along tear-bedewed trails. When their leaders saw the writing on the wall, they selected leading men of their tribe, well-seasoned and established stockmen and farmers, and sent them into the new country to select the land the Chickasaws would occupy.

The Chickasaws, a lowland people to begin with, took land which extended along the Red River above the Great Raft, beyond the Cross Timbers and into the open plains where the Kiowa and Comanche had their hunting grounds. Here was grass that would feed cattle as well as buffalo, and the Chickasaws became noted as stockmen. Many of them went into professions, and later were distinguished in state and local governments. Tales of the entertainments at the home of the wealthy Johnson family at Minco (the word means "Chief"), southwest of Oklahoma City, are still told with relish and nostalgia by their participants.

In the spring of 1971, the custom of appointing the principal chiefs of the Five Civilized Tribes was abolished by executive decree, and in the autumn of that year the first tribal elections in over one hundred years were held. Of the appointed chiefs, W. W. Keeler of the Cherokees, a Ross descendant, and Overton James of the Chickasaws were elected without great opposition. All other elections were bitterly contested.

Both Keeler and James are men of high education and proved executive ability, and it would be almost impossible to name another member of either tribe who could successfully oppose them.

Whatever became of the Osages, Otos and Quapaws, or the

Kiowas and Comanches, who were native to the land? They moved over, as far from the eastern tribes as their own habits and the local topography would let them, and went on living as much as they could as they had before. A distinct advantage of eastern Indian settlement to all of them was the availability of communities that could be raided. New opportunities for trade came into the country, and the western Indians, like the eastern ones, took advantage of them.

The Five Civilized Tribes had staked their claims in eastern Oklahoma and would never give them up, come hell, high water or civil war. The western Indians still had to put down their stakes.

CHAPTER 3

MAGIC DOGS, WOHAWS, IRON HORSES AND STEAMBOATS

The story of Oklahoma is not only the story of its settling, but of its unsettling. Max Cunningham, its first state highway engineer, who laid out what was basically the present system of main roads, once observed that Oklahoma was actually the only state to come into existence and to plan its highways after the coming of the automobile had changed the general pattern of American life. That was while Alaska and Hawaii were still territories. The same could be said of both of these states. In doing so, Max Cunningham compared Oklahoma to Los Angeles, the only major city of the United States of which the same thing is true. "Oklahomans will always be moving," he said more than once, and proved it by going on to construct a highway system in Louisiana and lay out the first Alcan Highway.

Mr. Cunningham should have known what he was talking about. He came to Oklahoma from Ohio by way of a draftsman's office in Chicago, as a railway surveyor, and he married a young woman whose family came from southern Indiana to "make the run" into the Cross Timbers. Mobility was his watchword.

But the pattern of mobility had been set for Oklahoma long before the internal combustion engine was invented. The Indian tribes native to western Oklahoma once lived in semisubterranean villages along the rivers or, when they went out on their seasonal hunting trips, in cone-shaped brush shelters that were the prototypes of their later buffalo-hide tipis.

When they moved from winter house to summer shelter the Plains Indians fastened harnesses around their dogs' bellies, attached drag poles to the harnesses and rawhide slings to the poles, and moved their possessions from place to place. In the northern plains the French *voyageurs* who first saw these drags called them *travois*, or carriers, and the word spread from tribe to tribe and is used by Indians and anthropologists alike to this day. It is like the ubiquitous word "squaw," which, originally used by the French to designate women of the loosest kind of morals, has gathered into itself an air of respectability and will, unfortunately, probably never be completely eradicated from the English language.

The drag dogs were large, and were specially bred for their job. Their use continued well into the 1800s, even after horses had largely replaced dogs as means of transportation. Breeding the dogs was purposeful and selective and was usually the work of women. That is one reason why we know so little about it; the earliest anthropologists to work in the plains were men who interviewed men, and like all men everywhere they recorded the histories of the Plains Indian tribes in terms of battles and of derring-do. It was not until women anthropologists entered the field that information about the daily lives and occupations of Plains Indian women began to be recorded and studied.

According to the data available to us from a Kiowa informant, who remembered the tellings of his mother and grandmothers, the preferred drag dogs of the short-grass country were about the size, conformation and color of a well-bred Boxer. Heavy chest and shoulder muscles were necessary to handle the loads and were developed both by breeding and by exercise. Often the drag dogs' tails were docked, to keep both dogs and loads cleaner. Even in 1973, it is inadvisable to take a good Boxer too near a good Kiowa. Alliances are easily formed.

A strange alteration in dog types occurred in western Oklahoma after 1870. Drag dogs had never been used for hunting, and even after horses replaced them as a means of transportation no Indian home was complete without its swarm of dogs. Officers posted to Fort Sill, Fort Reno, and Fort Supply brought their own hunting dogs with them. Soon the mounted cavalry learned that coyote hunting on the open plains was even more stimulating than fox hunting had been in the tame and well-fenced eastern states. They brought in fox hounds; then setters and pointers, and finally greyhounds, the only domesticated dogs that can run down coyotes. Some greyhounds wandered away from the posts and forgot their way back; others were borrowed and never returned. By 1900, the solid, intelligent, diligent and usually docile drag dog of the Plains Indians had almost completely disappeared. One or two old women continued dog breeding into the 1930s, but they are all gone now, and their work dogs with them. Still, every rural Indian family has its canine horde, strange mixtures of the imported with the original strains, generally with greyhound conformation predominating.

From purposefully breeding dogs, however, it was a short step to breeding horses. The first brood mares and stallions were brought into New Mexico by Oñate's colonists in 1580. Oñate had come north from Mexico to settle. He staked his claim and those of his followers in New Mexico, it is true. But it was only a little time before horses and mares found their way eastward, into Comanche and Kiowa hands, and they and the resulting colts remained Indian. Herds of wild horses—mustangs—ran the ranges as the horse population increased.

As has been said many times before, horses set the Plains people free. From the huddlers in semiunderground houses and brush shelters they became the dashing, colorful, warlike people that most non-Indians think and speak of as "typical Indians."

Once again, we know too little of the breeding of the animals. That it was to some extent planned and selective there can be no doubt. The Indians learned castration from the Spanish colonists or from the occasional Mexican traders —the *comancheros*—who ventured into the plains. Herds were culled, and soon mares, gelded stallions, and even worn-out war and hunting horses who had lost their speed and quickness of turning replaced the drag dogs almost entirely.

Stories of the dogs persisted, however, such as the one about the old couple who were too poor to have any horses, and who went behind the hunts the old man once had led, gathering scraps and offal that the members of the more active and prosperous families had disdained and discarded. Every scrap of meat was tied in a bundle made of rags of buffalo or deerhide, taken by drag dog to their shabby tipi and dried in the sun. If more prosperous families gave the old people game, only what they actually required to support life was eaten; the rest was dried with the scraps for later use.

Then, when winter came, and hunger coiled in the smoke that rose from fires where no cooking could be done because there was no food left from the summer, the old man could go through the village, calling,

"Mothers! Send us your little ones! Men! Send us your pregnant wives! Send us the people who most need food, for now is our time of plenty, and we have enough food for all!"

And the women and children came to be fed, and went away murmuring, "Aho! Aho!" in thanks for the kindness and generosity that had cared for them. This was the old couple's giveaway, to balance the gifts they had received from others during the summer.

Such stories are told today as examples of behavior for the young. The goodness of the old days will never be forgotten, nor will the fact that the old woman of the couple gave a well-trained dog to every woman who would promise to use it and care for it.

Everywhere in the plains, the Indians called horses "the magic dogs." Even though horses meant much more to the people than dogs ever had, in terms of wealth and status, animals that were so large and were capable of bearing men and women on their backs, as well as dragging loads, must be magical.

Horse trappings in the plains duplicated, unconsciously, Moorish-Spanish tack. The Indian saddle had a high pommel and a cantle that could serve as a back rest. Stirrup straps were long, with rawhide replacing tanned leather, and stirrups that duplicated as closely as possible the Spanish *tapaderos*, which were almost shoes.

There were nose bridles without bits, and there were braided rawhide halters, lariats, quirts and cruppers. Both the cruppers and the martingales that were worn by parade horses on festive occasions were elaborately quilled or beaded, and were as elegant as skill and taste could make them. Tassels of horsehair, metal pendants, or beaded medallions and, later, metal disks ornamented the head stalls. Strips of painted skin or brightly colored cloth were braided into the manes and tails of parade and war horses. Hunting horses were usually undecorated and were ridden bareback, with single lines from their nose halters.

There was a sharp distinction between the war horse, chosen principally for speed, the hunting horse, chosen for both speed and endurance, and the parade horse, chosen for show. It was the parade horse that gave rise to the legend that Plains Indians preferred to ride painted (pinto) horses. Selective breeding of pintos finally led to the development of the best-known American horse strain. This is the Appaloosa, a glorified pinto, which was first developed by the Nez Percés of the northern plains.

Pintos were bred and kept because, although they were supposed to be treacherous in disposition and as willing to throw a rider as to carry him, they were showy. Their hoofs could be weighted with rawhide bags filled with stones, so that they stepped high and bowed their necks, like show horses with steel-weighed hoofs in today's rings. Pintos were said to be controllable by one, or at most two, riders. They were never thought to be, in the truest sense of the word, reliably saddle-broken.

The preferred hunting and war horses were of solid colors—sorrel, bay, black or white. A black was generally believed to be too mettlesome for anything but a war charge, while a white horse could be trusted with the drags and was believed to be usually gentle and reliable in disposition and temperament. A roan or a dappled gray was good for either hunting or warfare or as a traveling horse. A woman or young boy could handle a dapple or a roan, even if it was a stallion.

Even better was the palomino (a light bay), sometimes almost golden in color, with white points, mane and tail, or the *bayo coyote* (the coyote bay), a light sorrel, bay or buckskin color, with dark points, mane and tail and a dark streak the length of its back.

Best of all, though, was the *grullo*, or blue, of an even blue-gray color without points. *Grullos* were believed to have bottomless endurance, courage and intelligence. Go to a horse race next week—if you can find a track where they race quarter horses, not Thoroughbreds, and bet on the blues. You'll come home smiling. These were the horses most Moors and Spaniards had preferred above all others, and these were the best of all horses to the Plains Indians and their successors, the cowmen.

War horses and hunting horses were painted with their owners' "power designs," symbols given in visions of supernatural beings, to assure fleetness and sureness of foot. Parade horses were held to be sufficiently decorated when they wore full trappings, although sometimes painted designs were added. A horse to be given to a friend usually bore the imprint of the giver's open hand on his hind quarters as a token of friendship.

Even women's drag horses, lowly though their state in life might be by male standards, often wore the same geometric designs the women painted on their rawhide containers or clothing.

Saddle making was usually the work of women. They chose

wooden crotches or the branches of antlers to be used for pommels and cantles: they split the wooden boards (usually of *bois d'arc* or Osage orange) that bound front to back along the horse's sides, and they laced the components together, covered the saddle tree with rawhide, and laced the wet skins in position to dry tightly and to make the saddle hard and firm. Kiowa women, in particular, took pride and pleasure in this work. They were superb saddlers, and they did not mind admitting it.

Of course the beadwork, quillwork and painting that decorated all horse trappings were also the work of women. From dogs they had progressed to horses, and we imagine that it was not long before they were advising the men on selective breeding, culling the herds they and the children took to and from pasture, and generally, if gently, directing the most masculine aspect of a supposedly man-dominated world. It's too bad some of those early anthropologists didn't listen to women on the subject of horses once in a while.

There was mobility east of the Timbers from the mid-eighteenth to mid-nineteenth centuries, too. Horses were essential to the dragoon troops posted to Fort Gibson from 1802 on, and to the lawmen of the Five Civilized Tribes. Each tribe had its troop of Light Horsemen, and while these mounted patrols could not be called by their enemies "the finest light cavalry in the world," as the Plains Indians were, they certainly were better than average for their day and time.

Unlike the Plains people, those of eastern Oklahoma rode European-style saddles, used metal horseshoes, and frequently indulged in horse-drawn carriages for their ladies and in wagons for farm work. They used horse-drawn plows. A road system of sorts worked itself out there almost automatically, usually paralleling the rivers. Women in eastern

Oklahoma rode sidesaddle, while the women of the plains rode astride.

In eastern Oklahoma, the flat pleasure-riding saddle was in vogue. Ordinarily these are called English saddles, but they are used as frequently in France, Italy and Germany as in England. Eventually, as the cattle business grew and there was need for carrying bedrolls, food, cooking utensils, tools, and lariats, the stock saddle and heavy duty work saddle became the cowman's choice throughout the West. The roping saddle, which is today called the western saddle, was adapted from Spanish and Mexican heavy gear and is in use now in places as far from the American West as Hawaii and New Zealand.

Horse breeding and handling, and the making of tack, was man's work in the country east of the Timbers. The Chickasaws, on their open-range lands along Red River, needed horses to work their cattle and came to excel as saddle makers. They, like other cattlemen, abandoned the English "postage stamp" in favor of the stockman's "rocking chair."

For working cattle, small, light, quick horses were necessary instead of the heavier Thoroughbreds, Morgans and Tennessee walking horses ridden east of the Timbers. A new strain worked itself out—the quarter horse—developed by crossing the heavier breeds with plains mustangs. Wherever cattle went so did quarter horses, from Texas to Montana and back by way of California, before the end of the nineteenth century.

Perhaps quarter-horse breeding was not purposefully selective, but it was soon clear that the offspring of these smaller horses tended to pick up the better qualities of both parents, and the strain was intentionally developed. To stand without hitching, the lines dropped to the ground from the headstall, while a man handled a calf; to pull back on the lariat and throw the horse's weight as well as the man's against that of a struggling "cow critter," and, most of all, "to turn on a dime and hand you a nickel's change" became the marks of the quarter horse. The name did not derive from the crossbreeding that went to produce the animal, but from the great bursts of speed over short distances—usually about a quarter of a mile. The quarter horse has endurance, too, and at a slower pace can cover a great deal of country in one day.

Quarter horses have come into their own in the last fifty years, not only as work horses but for racing, and anyone who has seen a cluster of them pounding down a track to the finish line can work up great admiration and affection for the lithe, speedy and well-formed beasts, regardless of their size.

The barrier of the Timbers ended in the Ozarks of Missouri. Beyond the mountains and trees, began the rolling prairies of western Missouri, Kansas, and the Oklahoma and Texas panhandles. By 1803, wagon trains were setting out from Independence, Missouri, crossing the plains and, by way of Cumbres Pass, reaching Taos, New Mexico.

Trade with New Mexico began in Taos, but the wagons rolled on south into the plaza of Santa Fe. There cottons, blankets, metal tools and utensils were exchanged for mountain furs, particularly beaver and buffalo hides.

It was not a particularly safe route, but it was one that was traveled persistently until 1870. The wagons were drawn by oxen, but the Santa Fe Trail was not to be confused with the later military and cattle trails, when these came into being. Its general direction was east to west, not north to south as the cattle trails went. Ruts in the sandy soil of the Oklahoma Panhandle, near Alva, still mark that crossing of the plains.

The discovery of the California gold fields in 1849 brought on a rush of transcontinental mobility everywhere, as people fought to reach the gold fields and their rich pickings.

In 1850, Captain Randolph Marcy, a West Pointer, an officer of dragoons, and a veteran of the Mexican War, was ordered from the relative quiet of his post at Fort Smith, Arkansas, to the outpost at Fort Towson in the Choctaw Nation, a few miles north of Red River. From there he was dispatched, with a small command, to map a southern route to California. The Sioux and the other tribes of the northern plains were harassing wagon trains and making travel by the northern route to California as difficult and unpleasant as they could. Of course, the Civilized Tribes wouldn't mind, said the War Department. Just draw up another treaty. Most of them are literate in English and can sign it.

As a matter of fact, the Choctaws and Chickasaws were not only unopposed to cross-country travel through their nations, they welcomed it. To the Choctaws, inveterate traders that they were, roads or river steamboat travel meant access to new sales outlets, while to the Chickasaws they meant easier travel to the stockyards and slaughter pens near Fort Gibson and Fort Smith.

Alidade in one hand, compass and notebook in the other, Marcy set out from Fort Towson in 1850. His men traveled light and lived off the country as much as they could. Marcy followed the westward Chickasaw trail along the Red River as far as possible. Then he packed up his alidade and put it away in favor of a hand ax when he encountered the Cross Timbers. He was one of the first, but not the last, of many explorers to pronounce them "virtually impassable."

But Marcy was a man of courage and determination. He was one of those who had trudged the Dead Man's Road across the Sonoran desert, on over the Sierra Madre to the valley of Mexico and the storming of Chapultepec Hill. He finally won his fight with the briars as he had his earlier struggle with Mexican cactus. He continued across the short-grass country of western Oklahoma, once he emerged from the Timbers. He was the first to map the landmarks of the rolling country and to give them official names. He noted the resemblances and differences among Kiowa, Comanche, Cheyenne and Arapaho, and could also catch their resemblances to the mounted tribes of the northern plains.

Marcy led his command across the Oklahoma and Texas panhandles, following the yucca stakes the Comanches and Plains Apaches had driven into the ground to mark the trails from water hole to water hole. Eventually he crossed the southern Rockies and Mohave Desert and stood, silent upon a peak in California, overlooking the Pacific Ocean, his ultimate goal.

Unlike his predecessors, Lewis and Clark and Zebulon Pike, Marcy had managed to hang onto and use his alidade and compass all the way. He not only produced an approximately complete map of the southwestern United States, he proved another point. The Cross Timbers might be "virtually impassable," but "virtually" did not mean "absolutely." Given sufficient determination a body of men could force their way through the woodlands, but not even Marcy recommended travel east to west or north to south through central Oklahoma. The area still remained a no man's land.

One thing was clear: If railroads could not go beyond the Indian nations they could go through north or south of them, through Texas, Missouri and Kansas. Soon the southern railroads were surveyed and transcontinental travel became a practical possibility. Only two things stood in the way of the iron horses in western Oklahoma: the buffalo and the flashing, fighting Indians who lived from the herds.

The railroads hired professional hunters to eliminate the buffalo herds. That this also meant eliminating most of the Indians was a matter of only incidental interest to the railroad tycoons, as they were beginning to call themselves. Passengers on some of the early trains carried their own rifles, or borrowed arms from one another or from members of the train crews, to indulge in the sport of buffalo—and sometimes Indian—shooting.

The meat of the slaughtered animals was salvaged by the Indians or allowed to rot beside the tracks, but the hides had commercial value. Boston and other Atlantic seaboard cities were busy tanning hides and manufacturing shoes and horse equipment, so trains that might otherwise have returned empty from California were soon sent back loaded with "flint" hides—skins sun dried with the hair on—ready to undergo the lengthy processes of commercial tanning.

And then there were the bones. As the meat fell away from them, it became apparent that an excellant source of organic fertilizer was strewn all over the ground and going to waste. "Bone wagons" went out collecting; soon the bones piled beside the tracks for loading and shipping rose above the stations' eaves.

The Indians east of the Timbers were civilized—everybody said so—and they could see the potential value of hides and bones as well as any white man. Their relations with the United States Government were conducted through federal agents stationed in the five national capitals. The eastern tribes had welcomed the railroads and also welcomed the great cattle trails that soon crossed the country north to south, paralleling the Timbers on either side, and providing a means of reaching railheads in Kansas and Missouri.

Even before the railroads began surveying and construction, in Oklahoma proper, the cattle herds were blazing their own trails. The Great Western Trail ran from Fort Worth, Texas, and its surrounding country, north to the Red River at Doan's Store or Doan's Crossing (both names were used) and on north to Dodge City, Kansas. The Chisholm Trail, east of the Great Western and running in places along the edge of the Timbers, crossed from central Texas at Red River Station and forked just north of the Cimarron River in central Oklahoma. One branch ran west to Dodge City, while the other swerved a little to the east and the railhead at Wichita, Kansas. The Shawnee Trail brought cattle from the *bosques* of eastern Texas to Colbert's Ferry on the Red River in the Choctaw Nation. Farther north it, too, forked at Boggy Depot, the West Shawnee Trail running almost due north along the eastern margin of the Timbers to Wichita, Kansas, while the East Shawnee Trail, which supplied Fort Gibson in Indian Territory and Fort Smith in Arkansas, terminated at Baxter Springs, Kansas.

Probably, thanks to writers of "Westerns" and to television, Dodge City is the best known of the railheads and its reputation is the most unsavory. However, all the cow towns were rough and ready, and Wichita and Baxter Springs were no more places to hold Sunday-school reunions than was Dodge City.

The most exposed and dangerous trails were the Great Western and the Chisholm. They followed open country and available water; cattle could be walked slowly along them and put on weight in the process; calf wagons could follow the herds to attend to obstetrical emergencies and carry the bawling offspring to their mothers for feeding, but in spite of these advantages there were the Indians.

Both trails passed through Comanche, Kiowa, Apache, Cheyenne and Arapaho country, and attacks on cattle droves were as frequent as attacks on the wagon trains that crossed westward from Independence, Missouri, through Kansas and the Oklahoma and Texas panhandles, over Cumbres Pass, and into Taos and Santa Fe, New Mexico.

Indeed, a little friendly blackmail often marked the progress of a cattle drive or wagon train. Indians would appear in full war panoply, drawn up for attack. Then one of their leaders would ride forward to demand tribute in the form of "wohaws" or trade goods before the trains could pass. Wohaw was the word used universally in the plains to designate cattle. It probably derived from the wagoners' cries of "Whoa! Haw!" to the oxen.

The cattle trails as such have been obliterated, covered with concrete and asphalt and forming part of Mr. Cunningham's road system. Why, said that practical man, do more surveying than was actually necessary, especially in country so obviously unsuited for anything but the range cattle industry anyway? Nobody would be fool enough to try to plow and plant western Oklahoma; at most it would support one cow per twenty-five acres, and that would mean a human population of such low density that only a few roads would be needed. Chickasha, Verden, Anadarko, Carnegie and Hobart could be linked through to the east by a straight-line highway to Norman, Tecumseh and Seminole. It is with wry humor that one of Mr. Cunningham's nieces looks at the carpet factories, automobile trailer factories, lakes and boat docks and grain elevators that dot the landscape today. Not to mention Guymon's stock pens and slaughterhouses.

The first straight-line dirt road is now paralled to the south by the H. E. Bailey Turnpike, the state's most expensive to drive, which runs from Oklahoma City via Fort Sill and Lawton to the Texas line. To the north, old Highway 9 is paralleled by Interstate 40, once Highway 66 and "the main street of America" between Chicago and Los Angeles.

Meanwhile, back to the east of the Cross Timbers, a new industry was developing, water transportation. The Great Raft had been blasted out of existence in 1880 and the Arkansas River opened to the Three Forks, where the Illinois and Grand rivers flowed into it at Fort Gibson. Shallow draft boats and barges could come upriver from the Mississippi, and many occupants of eastern Oklahoma preferred the more leisurely voyage by steamer to the difficulties of horse travel to the railroad, and so east.

One of the great lost statistics of history is the number of pianos the boats brought upriver from New Orleans. Why the pianos always came from New Orleans is also unknown, except for the possibility that the first ones came for the young ladies of leading Choctaw and Chickasaw families—the Leflores, the Colberts, the Maytubbys and the Lanes—who had married into Louisiana French families.

Anyway, the pianos came, and with them Sèvres china, fine silver from England, ornamental glassware from Venice and Prague, and a quantity of objects that adorned life in the leading families. In 1965, the writers undertook the conversion of the Union Agency, at Muskogee, into a Five Civilized Tribes Museum. Baskets, pottery and wooden utensils came to light from attics and basements of the

Cherokee, Choctaw, Creek and Seminole, and some very valuable specimens were contributed to the museum.

But nowhere could we find anything representative of the Chickasaw. At last a tribal leader invited us to select from his personal collection of eighteenth-century *mille fleurs* French paperweights, Sèvres *pots de chambres*, copper cooking utensils clearly showing the marks of their makers in Birmingham, England, a Cheyenne war bonnet which had been presented to him because of his interest in Indian affairs, and the officer's sword and cavalry pistol his grandfather had fought with in the Confederate Army.

"Nothing that came over the Trail of Tears?" we wailed, already so soaked by the other four that we could think of nothing but weeping.

"Ladies," the tribal leader reminded us, "the Chickasaws never traveled a Trail of Tears. We came in our own way and at our own expense."

Crushed, we accepted the Confederate weapons to ornament the Chickasaw case.

Actually, it was during the Civil War that travel on the eastern rivers became really important. Munitions and supplies were brought upriver to the Confederate sympathizers in all Five Tribes. Afterward the traffic declined, although pleasure boats left Muskogee landing for Webbers Falls, Oklahoma, and Fort Smith, Arkansas, as late as 1910. By then a whole series of railroads crisscrossed eastern Oklahoma, and river travel was abandoned. The ever-shallow streams silted up, dams and reservoirs were constructed on all three rivers north of the Three Forks, and Oklahoma became again a landlocked state.

In the 1950s, Senator (formerly Govenor) Robert S. Kerr began introducing bills into the United States Congress to reopen the rivers to "the Port of Catoosa," a small community north and east of Tulsa. Rail travel had almost ceased for passenger trains, replaced by air and bus transport, and railroad lines were merging, going out of business or raising their freight rates astronomically. River transportation for bulky freight would be more economical than rail carriage, and eventually the senator proved his point. On January 22, 1971, ten years after Senator Kerr's death, a bargeload of newsprint out of Greeneville, Tennessee, was unloaded at the Port of Muskogee—again at the Three Forks. President Richard M. Nixon dedicated the site, at the invitation of Republican Governor Dewey Bartlett. Pleasure and houseboats were already using the Arkansas, and on January 24, 1971, the Port of Catoosa was formally dedicated by Democratic Governor David Hall, his first official act.

We shall have a great deal more to say about Oklahoma, water and the Army Corps of Engineers in a later chapter. For the present it is enough to say that Oklahoma is no longer landlocked.

CHAPTER 4

WARPATHS AND BATTLES

Besides practicing blackmail on cattle drives across their hunting lands, the Indians of western Oklahoma put up an armed struggle. They were not going to sit down meekly and accept the reservation system.

At one time the commandant at Fort Supply, in the northwest corner of the state, reported that the Cheyennes and Arapahos were better armed, better equipped and better mounted than his men. In 1856, it seemed expedient to build a line of frontier outposts along the western margin of the Timbers, in order to hold the western tribes in check. Similar forts had previously been constructed along the Texas-Mexico border.

Construction in Indian Territory, as eastern Oklahoma was beginning to be known, began at Fort Arbuckle, near the present town of Davis. It extended west and north from there through what later became Oklahoma Territory, to what is now Fort Sill, on to Fort Reno, at El Reno, and to Camp (later, Fort) Supply in the Panhandle, which was only a hundred miles from Dodge City and the railroad, and therefore could be used as a supply depot for the other outposts. Hence its name.

From Dodge City it was easy to reach Fort Riley, the Army remount station and southwestern headquarters, in Kansas. The plan was carefully worked out, and it seemed to be working, when the first mutterings of Civil War were heard. Probably the military stationed at the outposts were not greatly interested in politics on the east side of the Mississippi. Some officers were slaveowners, but they, like most Southerners, took Negro slavery for granted.

But when war came, it came with a bang—literally, at Fort Sumter, South Carolina. Troops were recalled from the frontier, and the Indians on the plains resumed their old carefree ways.

They now had Texas settlements and settlers to prey on, and could suspend hostilities among themselves while they raided southward to the Rio Grande. The Civil War gave the Plains Indians a brief period of renewed glory, without interruptions from the "blue coat soldiers," and their "see-far glasses."

In eastern Oklahoma, matters went differently. Some members of the Five Civilized Tribes were slaveholders who had brought their chattels west with them. Not only Indians wept their way along the trails of tears. Slavery continued as an established institution; slaves were bred, sold and traded, and a cotton-based economy rested largely on sweating black backs. Here, the men who owned slaves had every intention of keeping them, and of fighting for what they considered their rights and possessions.

On the other hand, there were those among the members of the Five Civilized Tribes who opposed slavery. No man, in their view, could ethically own another. So the tribes split down the middle, half Confederate, half Union, in sympathy. Feuds began then that are still to be resolved. Enmities developed, to be continued in the politics of the 1970s.

It is generally said in eastern Oklahoma, that all the Five Tribes "went with the South." That was not the case. According to Mark Twain, there are "liars, damn liars, and statistics," and in this case we must rely on the statistics. These show that equal numbers of Indians from eastern Oklahoma served with the Union and Confederate armies.

Surprisingly enough, the Light Horsemen of the Five Tribes formed the frontier bumper that the Union badly needed at that time. They held the posts the military had abandoned and checked the eastward ravages of the western tribes. Better frontier guards never rode, and it is due to the Light Horsemen that the western tribes were contained as well as they were.

Texas had joined the Union, and then seceded from it, and there were plenty of Texans who took refuge in the Indian nations to the northeast when the going got too tough in the West. The Light Horsemen could not protect all of Texas—nobody could, not even the heroes of the Alamo who went down before Mexican gunfire—but what they could do along the Red River to protect and shelter refugees from the southern state, the Light Horsemen did. Many Texans took up Indian lands by squatters' rights, and stayed north of the Red River when the war was over.

It would be too much to say that Oklahoma's contributions to the Civil War were noteworthy. A Cherokee, General Stand Watie, with the Confederacy, was the only Indian to reach general officer's status in the nineteenth century, and even he finally went down in defeat at the Battle of Big

Cabin Creek, the only Civil War battle actually fought in Oklahoma. Pea Ridge was a battle in which Watie's troops participated, but that was over the line in Arkansas, and so didn't count.

By the time the war was over, it was apparent that more than frontier outposts were needed in the West. Camp Radziwill became Fort Sill, with the buildings that surrounded its parade ground constructed of massive native stone. Lawton, the inevitable "post town," grew up four miles south of Fort Sill. Fort Reno, a day's hard horseback ride north of Sill, was also strengthened, and its "post town," El Reno, later became a division point on the Rock Island Railroad. Fort Supply and its town, Cantonment, now had a sidetrack of their own from Dodge City. Wagon trains rolled across the plains again, and so did the blue-coat soldiers.

Many of these soldiers were Negroes, commanded by white officers. The end of the war had freed all blacks, and many of the young men, landless, without trades or experience, and with freedom a heady taste in their mouths, joined the Army. Here they had quarters, like everybody else; food, like everybody else, and best of all, paydays like everybody else. Who cared if their officers were white or black? The whites had always commanded. This was nothing new.

Often the Negro servicemen had begun life as slaves in the Five Civilized Tribes. Freed or escaped, they joined the Union forces, as much for revenge as for economic reasons. To them, Indians were Indians and the freedmen rode them down with a combination of desperation and triumph.

The Ninth and Tenth Cavalry regiments were entirely Negro in enlisted and non-commissioned personnel. These "buffalo soldiers," or "black white men"—the Indians used

1. Arapaho School, Darlington, Oklahoma, June 26, 1891.
   Courtesy of Oklahoma Historical Society.

2. Ferry at union of Grand and Arkansas rivers, 1894.
   Courtesy of Oklahoma Historical Society.

3. At the Registration Booth, Arkansas City, before the run into central Oklahoma, April 21, 1889.
Courtesy of Oklahoma Historical Society.

4. Sod house in Oklahoma, 1896.
Courtesy of Oklahoma Historical Society.

5. The graduating class of 1895, Chilocco Industrial School, Oklahoma Territory.
Courtesy of Oklahoma Historical Society.

both names in referring to them—were the scourge of the Plains Indians. They had literally nothing to lose and everything to gain by acquiring a good military reputation. And acquire it they did. Next to the Light Horsemen they were the toughest, hardest riding organized bodies of troops on the plains.

Not only displaced Negroes came into the plains; their officers were frequently men who had served in the Civil War and found it difficult, even sometimes impossible, to settle into civilian life. Sherman, Sheridan, the Custers, the soldier's soldier George Crook, and his Boswell, John Bourke, were only some of the general officers who served with more or less distinction in western Oklahoma.

The first order of the day was to round up, disarm and squash the Indians, and battles began to be fought in earnest in the West. The Battle of the Washita, north of Cheyenne, Oklahoma, is probably the best known, and is the classic example of Colonel George Custer's stupidity, sadism and greed. Undoubtedly it led to his death, six years later, at the Battle of the Little Big Horn in Montana. Even Custer's troops shed tears at the beauty of the objects they were ordered to destroy in Black Kettle's Camp on the Washita, but if beauty were in the eyes of some beholders, it was lacking in the Colonel's. Custer's defense was that of the officers tried for the My Lai massacre in the 1970s—he was a soldier obeying orders.

The Kiowas fled out onto the staked plains, and with them went many of the Comanches. The Apaches scattered like blown cottonwood leaves before a high wind and disappeared, to turn up later with Geronimo's raiders in Arizona. Ironically, it was at Apache, Oklahoma, near Fort Sill, that

Geronimo ended his days, technically a prisoner in a strange, rolling land unlike the soaring peaks of the White Mountains among which he had been born, in Arizona.

Sitting Bear, White Bear and Big Tree had led the Kiowa forces. When they were captured, first Sitting Bear and later White Bear chose suicide over life in a federal prison. Only Big Tree survived imprisonment and returned, chastened and Christianized, to his people. "He never was much," said one of White Bear's descendants, referring to Big Tree a century later. "He just went along with the real men."

To be a real man: that was the deepest ambition of every Plains Indian male. A real man stood up for what he believed; he did not compromise. So some of the Kiowas and Comanches, the Wichitas and Caddoes who had been marched south from Kansas and north from the Texas Gulf Coast, with hardships unknown to any of the Five Civilized Tribes, could accept such a man as Thomas C. Battey.

Quaker missionary and teacher, Thomissey, as the Indians called Battey, spoke always with a straight tongue, even when he counseled against revolt and warfare with the whites.

For war was not confined to the southern plains. It swept from Minnesota to the Pacific as well. The Oregon Modocs resisted all efforts to be confined to reservations and took refuge in the knife-edge blackness of their lava beds until they were starved into surrender. This happened about the same time that Sitting Bear, White Bear and Big Tree made their last desperate struggle for freedom.

Thomissey was a friend of Kicking Bird, the Kiowa peace chief, and it was to Kicking Bird he went when word of the Modocs' murder of peace commissioners, who were also Quaker missionaries, reached him. At the request of the United States Government, Thomissey attempted to reconcile the divided Kiowas, and to bring peace to the southern plains. Otherwise, said "Woosinton," the Kiowas would be held captive until matters were settled with the Modocs.

Thomissey was a desperately sick man when he went from the Caddo School and Agency at what was to be Anadarko, Oklahoma, to Kicking Bird's camp on Stinking Water (now more politely called Medicine Bluff) Creek. Part of the way he traveled by army ambulance, but when the pain inside him became unbearable he left that jolting conveyance and walked.

"He always was a great walker and a great talker," his daughter told us when we visited her. The old lady—she was then approaching one hundred with all the zest with which she had approached ten—added that she knew her father suffered from ulcers at that time, and that perhaps he then felt the first gnawing of the cancer that ultimately killed him.

At any rate, Thomissey outtalked even White Bear, no mean feat in conversation with "The Orator of the Plains" and persuaded the Kiowas to remain at peace with the whites —for the time being. The problem was that the Kiowas knew they were being threatened with punishment for something somebody else had done, but they had no more heard of the Modocs than the Modocs had heard of them, and it seemed to the Kiowas they were being threatened with one more injustice.

Soon afterward Thomissey's health forced him to return to his home in Iowa, to the wife and family whom he had pulled himself away from when he "heard the Call," and to settle down to teaching school and writing his memoirs—*A Quaker's Adventures Among the Indians*. The book was submitted to the Society of Friends in Philadelphia, where an editorial board removed all mention of the Modoc "atrocities," and released a volume that left at least one reader in a perpetual state of wonder until the University of Oklahoma Press published a reprint edition, for which she was asked to write an introduction. Then the mystery of Thomissey's final journey to Kicking Bird's camp was at last resolved, for Thomissey's granddaughter produced the original manuscript of the missing chapter, and it was restored to its rightful place in the book.

Men like Thomissey and the Quaker peace commissioners the Modocs shot down in the lava beds were the real heroes of the Indian wars. Nelson Miles, another Quaker teacher and missionary, was appointed Indian agent at Darlington, near Fort Reno, and while he could not persuade all the Cheyennes to stay in Oklahoma and be good little Indians, he did prevent all but Dull Knife's band from escaping the dust, heat and awful monotony of an Oklahoma reservation for the faraway Big Horn Mountains of Wyoming and Tongue River of Montana. But that tragic flight is a story of Montana and Nebraska, not Oklahoma.

And the Modocs? What to do with the Modocs? Why remove them to Oklahoma, of course, which was rapidly becoming a dumping ground for all kinds of Indians. They were settled in the northeastern part of the state, where it was hoped hills and rivers would make them feel at home, on lands the Cherokee Nation had ceded (for a price) for the settlement of a jar of mixed Indian pickles: Senecas, Wyandots, Weas, Wacos, Piankashas, Delawares, Tonkawas and Modocs, around Vinita and Miami, Oklahoma.

It was too much. The Modocs, too, disliked heat and mosquitoes and strangers. They were and are loners, as a people. They stubbornly insisted on being taken back to Oregon, and eventually they won their point. Back to

Klamath Lake, back to Sprague River, back to the Pacific Cascade Mountains they went, and the government paid their rail fare. A Modoc woman once told one of us that they were "the only people who ever licked Woosinton."

CHAPTER 5

RUN, RUN, RUN FOR YOUR LIVING

Under their own laws and their treaties with the United States Government, the Five Civilized Tribes held absolute control of their lands. They had codified laws, trained lawyers and a law enforcement body. They could admit or refuse admittance to anyone who was not Indian but wished to transact business, teach school or open a mission in eastern Oklahoma. The Indian Territory, as it came to be known after the Civil War, and its Indian citizens were autonomous.

All Five Tribes were proud of the loyalty, honesty and integrity of their members, of whatever factions. The story is told from tribe to tribe of a man who quarreled with another and shot him. The murderer, tried by tribal court, was sentenced to death by shooting by a member of the victim's family. It was in the spring of the year, and the crops had just gone into the ground. The man to be executed was allowed to go home for the summer, get his crops cultivated and harvested and return on his word of honor for execution in the fall. In October he duly reported to the tribal court and was duly shot. At least one of the "execution trees" to which condemned men were bound stands in the square surrounding the Creek Council House at Okmulgee.

Another favorite story, and again it could have happened anywhere, in any tribe, is told of a traveling salesman who took shelter from a storm with an Indian family and was hospitably urged to spend the night. After dinner, when he was ready to go to bed, the white man wound his watch and cached it under his pillow.

"What makes you do that?" his Indian host inquired. "There isn't another white man in fifty miles."

The expression passed into folklore unchanged and is in use by most Oklahomans today.

Wagon trains, cattle drives, railroads and, after the Civil War, river boats were rapidly opening up the country. Illinois, Iowa, Indiana, Kentucky, Nebraska and Missouri were filling up with farmers and stockmen; with small industries and the professional services needed in every community. There were too many leftover Indians in these states, and a place had to be found to put them. They were woodland peoples to begin with. Why not settle them in the Cross Timbers, with which perhaps they could cope?

The decision to do so was reached in 1870. The Osage, Oto, Ponca, Quapaw and everybody's traditional enemies, the Pawnees, could move over—maybe out onto the plains. They were as much horticulturalists as they were hunters, and they probably could scratch out a living anywhere, by some means. Once more they shifted a hundred miles to the west.

The Cherokees again ceded (for a price, in 1866) a strip extending westward on either side of the Kansas border. This was a good place for the quasi Plains tribes, especially the

Osage and Oto, who were inclined to be rambunctious at best, and who had always claimed the salt beds near Alva, Oklahoma, at the western end of the Cherokee strip, as their own. Of course the Cherokees had asked for the western extension because of the salt beds, but they had others in the Cookson Hills and along the Illinois River drainage—the Three Forks area was famous for its salt beds—so the Cherokees turned the western deposits over to the Osages, who had so far prevented Cherokee access to the salt in any case.

It was not until surveying of the lands to be occupied by the northeastern tribes began that it was discovered that the Cross Timbers had never been surveyed or mapped. How could they have been? Randolph Marcy was probably the only man of his day capable of doing such a survey, and Marcy had other things on his mind when he battled the Timbers.

So there it was, a lovely hole in the map, right in the middle of the United States, up for grabs. The Indians were not yet settled in the area, and nobody had laid claim to any of it. The Cross Timbers were available, as the lands of the Mississippi drainage had been to Union veterans after the Civil War. The same homestead laws that applied to the veterans could apply to other homesteaders just as well.

The man who saw the possibilities first was a jack-of-all-trades and master of none, presently employed as clerk in the Department of Interior. His name was David Payne. Settlement of the lands west of the Indian Territory was his first attempt to organize anything.

Payne left his job in Washington. He traveled, somehow—probably often at other people's expense—through Illinois, Iowa and particularly through Kansas. He gathered together men like himself, displaced, not outright failures but not howling successes, either, and brought them, with their families, into the lands west. Many of Payne's followers were Kansans, wheat farmers who did not have enough land in their own state to raise wheat in paying quantities, now that machine plowing and harvesting had begun.

Payne made one oversight, and it was characteristic of the man. He forgot or blithely ignored the fact that land had to be opened for settlement by Act of Congress or presidential decree, and neither had been enacted as far as the central Oklahoma lands were concerned. Undeterred by legal technicalities, Payne led his people southward into his promised land.

People were living when we began work on this book who had been among Payne's Boomers (they were booming down into new country, which is why they were called the Boomers). Their stories have been collected and recorded; the state rejoices in archives hither and yon, and some contain very valuable material.

As one woman told the story, there was a charm in the western Oklahoma air.

"David Payne was a handsome man," she said. "One look at those blue eyes of his, and you knew he could move mountains."

It was the spring of 1873, and up through the rolling short-grass country that bordered the Timbers on the west, where Payne's settlers entered Oklahoma, came a carpet of wild flowers: gaillardias, burgundy cups, poppy mallows, white and pink and gold; the blue and white lupinlike drapes of the locoweed, the little pink and blue grass starflowers, sunflowers, milkweed, the white flames of yucca candles, and the drooping greeny-white blossoms of chinaberries. Redbuds and white haws followed the streams, and in the open country the wild sand plums sent out their breadlike fragrance. Over it all arched a sky of incredible turquoise blue, sometimes splashed with white thunderheads or blackened with coming storms. At night you could reach up and pull down stars from the blue-black of the sky. And as summer wore on, gold dominated other flower colors, coreopsis and sunflowers took over everything. In the fall the leaves turned, not red like eastern trees except the sumac, but the pale gold of cottonwoods and elms, and the luminescence of ripe chinaberries.

Some of the flowers still survive in pasture lands, but others are gone. Locoweed was beautiful, but as soon as its effect on cattle and horses became known, it was ruthlessly rooted out. The pink and blue starflowers and the spreading lapis spiderworts were trampled down and grazed over and vanished. Flowers that one remembers as commonplace in 1917 and were even more lavish earlier are gone now. Since few botanists in earlier years paid any attention to the plants, only their common names are known by most elderly contemporary Oklahomans. Industrial pollution has darkened the skies and the stars are out of reach except by space-ship travel.

David Payne looked at the land in 1886 and saw that it was good, but the military posted to Fort Reno and Fort Sill looked at David Payne at this same time and saw, not the faith that moves mountains, but an intruder on lands where they were barely holding the Indians under control at best. It was not, in military minds, the best time or place for strangers, and especially not for strangers who wanted to settle and farm.

So the military moved, and before them, leisurely, for there were women and children in the covered wagons, moved

Payne's Boomers. Children grew tanned, and pretty girls freckled, and fathers and mothers ceased worrying about dangers from Indians, cowboys or soldiers. Before the frost dusted the rolling land in October, friendships and even marriages had been formed between the two constantly moving groups.

The Boomers traveled south from Kansas, by way of Fort Supply, to Fort Reno, on their own. Then, gently but firmly urged forward by the blue-coat men, they moved on, across the Washita, almost to Medicine Bluff Creek. There the Fort Reno troops turned back to their base. The Fort Sill military body came out to meet the Boomers, and began unobtrusively to escort them back to Fort Reno.

Payne had gone back to Washington, and was trying in every way he knew to push a land opening bill through Congress. The real leader of the Boomers during the forced migrations back and forth across the plains was Glenn Couch, hardy and shrewd, but without the dynamic personal quality that distinguished Payne. Couch had stick-to-itiveness, though, and that was more needed than charm at the moment.

The idyllic summer of 1886, with its Sunday stops for rest and worship, singing hymns to a melodeon carried in one of the wagons, a sermon from the chaplain and prayers from anybody who felt like praying or testifying, ended before winter's first blasting blue norther. The Boomers squatted on the fringes—and ragged fringes they were—of Liberal, Kansas, and waited for the final word to come from Washington. When it came, it was devastating. Payne was dead of pneumonia.

Payne's land opening bill passed Congress and was signed into law by President Grover Cleveland in February of 1889, though Payne was no longer alive to enjoy the victory. This bill opened a section of Unassigned Lands—as they were formerly referred to—which included the present counties of Logan, Oklahoma, Cleveland, Canadian, Kingfisher and Payne, where the cities of Stillwater, Oklahoma City, Norman, Guthrie, Kingfisher and El Reno are located.

The prospective settlers were held by the Army on the north side of the Kansas line for a week. It was a time of wild excitement, of gambling on horses whose owners were foolish enough to risk the wind and stamina of their mounts on such foolishness; of buying and selling of food and water at almost prohibitive rates; of retiring wagon wheels and reshoeing horses. Lawyers assured prospective clients that the attorneys would be available to register land claims as soon as offices could be set up in the town sites. One hundred sixty acres of woodland or one city block in a town site went to each winner of the race. Railroad engines stood waiting, ready to make the run at a footpace so that prospective claimants could drop off when they saw a likely place. There were high-wheeled bicycles to be ridden through the brush as well as they could be. Riding horses, buggies, farm wagons—all were lined up. The same scene was repeated at the Chickasaw Nation border to the south.

"Oh, Joe! Here's your mule!" heralded the arrival of any one of several bootleggers. The white-lightning whiskey they peddled was known to kick like a mule. The expression is still in more or less common use in that section of Oklahoma.

At exactly noon on April 22, an army bugle sounded "To the Colors," a cannon boomed, the soldiers dropped to the ground with the ropes they had been holding to keep the mob in line, and the run was on.

Czechoslovakian and Irish immigrants, the displaced and

unemployed of eastern cities, the lashin's and lavin's of railroad and construction crews, English gentlemen out for a lark, a whole community from French Indiana—all swept forward into the Indian lands where they would drive their stakes before the day's end. Even a few Cherokees and Choctaws joined in the rush, some of them hoping for appointments at the Indian agencies, others for surplus lands.

It was a wild scramble. From north and south the claimants met at Oklahoma Station—now Oklahoma City—for a time the only post office in Oklahoma Territory.

There were fights, of course. Many were brushes with the "Sooners"; those who had sneaked in and staked claims before the official opening. The people who had come in legally called themselves "Boomers"; they started when the cannon boomed. What had been a dirty name when applied to Payne's followers became respectable, and in time "Sooner" would gain respectability also.

CHAPTER 6

PREPARING FOR THE FUTURE

In 1892, another land opening took place, north and west of the lands homesteaded in 1889. In the same year the surplus lands of the Cheyennes and Arapahos were opened without cession, and Clinton, Arapaho, Cheyenne, Erick, Calumet and Sayre came into being. The still rebellious Indian troublemakers had been active participants in the Ghost Dance which swept Nevada and the northern plains in 1891, and they had to be punished somehow. Opening their lands to settlement was one way of doing it.

If homesteading in the Cross Timbers had its problems, homesteading in the short-grass country had other and different ones. Here there was far less water than in the lands to the east or in the Timbers, and much of what there was, was brackish with gypsum. The wind swept across the plains, as the song says, but it never seemed to stop sweeping, and as soon as plows ripped open the soil, dust swept with the wind.

But this was plains country, and the plains country of

the more northern Middle Western states was the breadbasket of the world. Western Oklahoma, therefore, must at least supply rolls, if not loaves. It did yield much grain at first, unfortunately. Later the exhausted soil refused to yield anything but cockleburrs and tumbleweeds. The settlers, who lived in dugouts scooped out along creek banks or in sod houses built with blocks of grassy-bound earth, were determined to prove their point. They took their problems out in song:

> DOWN ON THE CLAIM
> Picking up bones to keep from starving,
> Picking up chips to keep from freezing,
> Picking up courage to keep leaving,
> Way out West, in No Man's Land.

(The chips referred to in this ditty are flat dry cakes of buffalo or cow manure, and make excellent clean smokeless fuel.)

Because the eastern states were already being devastated by an economic depression, many of the men who rode the rails to the western openings had once been part of the riffraff of the cities. This was their chance to join the respectable small-town element among the settlers and to rehabilitate themselves on land of their own. Certain points of etiquette, naturally, were observed on both sides.

> WHAT WAS YOUR NAME?
> What was your name in the States?
> Was it Thompson or Johnson or Bates?
> Did you murder your wife and fly for your life?
> Say, what was your name in the States?

As late as 1920 it was a fearful breach of good manners to ask anyone his name. "If he wants you to know, he'll tell you."

And there was yet another song of the West, wherever lands were homesteaded, that took a matter-of-fact approach to the problems of pioneer life, and described them with unflinching accuracy:

THE LITTLE OLD SOD SHANTY

I'm looking rather seedy now while holding down my claim,
My vittles are not always the best,
And the mice they play around me as I nestle down to rest,
In my little old sod shanty on the claim.
    Oh, the hinges are of leather and the windows
       have no glass,
    The boards, they let the howling blizzards in—
    You can see the hungry coyote as he sneaks up
       thru the grass,
    To my little old sod shanty on the claim.

In all there were thirteen separate land openings in western Oklahoma, the last being the Big Pasture in the southwest. These were lands which had not been allotted to the Kiowa, Comanche, Wichita and Caddo tribes. This took place in 1906, a year before statehood. In some cases lands were claimed by lottery instead of runs. Names of prospective settlers were filed at the government land offices, and on the day of a drawing the names of the winners were read from slips of paper shaken in a drum. The drawings continued until all the available land and town sites had been claimed. The town sites were already laid out on a grid, and all the lucky winner had to do first was put up a tent and get in business. He still had to prove legal ownership and improvements. Law offices, drugstores, doctors' offices, churches and groceries all operated out of tents for months sometimes, until permanent buildings could be erected.

Land opening bills specified that the land was available for "white" settlement. A group of Negroes from eastern Tennessee, who had banded together in covered wagons to make the journey to the Cheyenne and Arapaho opening, were denied permission to take up claims, because they were not white. Sadly, they returned to the farms they had abandoned.

Later, land that had been claimed and had proved unprofitable for farming was sold to Negroes or leased to them as tenant farmers. Many of the Negro farmers proved more adept at working the soil than their white neighbors. They were alert to the native plants, cultivated wild plum and choke cherry trees and put in truck gardens that supplied the nearby towns with much-needed fresh produce.

Building west of the Timbers was a problem until the invention of poured concrete structures and of geodesic domes. Wood or brick had to be shipped in, and shipping costs were high. There was plenty of local stone, but dynamiting it out of its strata was costly and dangerous. Some towns in eastern Oklahoma and southern Kansas were blessed with clay beds, and in these communities bricks could be fired and sent to those lucky enough to have the means to pay for them.

Among the best-known clay beds were Chandler and Stroud, first in Indian Territory and later in Oklahoma Territory (these bricks are stamped Chandler I.T. and Stroud, I.T.), Bristow in Indian Territory and Coffeyville in Kansas. Oklahoma City has its brick plant still, north and west of its original location. It was moved when the clay supply ran low. Perhaps the most famous brick turned out in the area was the "Don't Spit on Sidewalk" brick. It is said to have been laid during an influx of tuberculois patients about 1900, and was placed in front of the Opera House on the Main Street of Guthrie. These bricks have become collectors' items since they were replaced with asphalt paving, and one of the writers of this book proudly displays her "Don't Spit" as a book end.

From the beginning there had been ladies in eastern Oklahoma. Many of the upper-class women of the Five Civilized Tribes were educated in the East, abroad, or in their own national seminaries. They read novels and ladies' magazines; they played the ubiquitous pianos, they embroidered, they even painted clusters of flowers on china, treasure boxes and other small *objets d'art*. And they were not only "cultured ladies" in the usual limited sense of the word, they were intelligent, capable women, who could hold their own in conversation with anybody and were appalled by the outlaws, bandits, hold-up men and bootleggers who drifted into Indian Territory from Kansas, Arkansas and Texas.

But unlike Indian Territory, Oklahoma Territory was largely a man's world. Many women there inhabited the "cat houses" along the railheads or were too busy with their share of scratching out claims and the hard work that holding claims entailed to have time for ladylike airs and graces. Women, respectable women, were at a premium.

In 1904, young Sydney Cunningham, from Chicago, visiting her brother Max, and in every sense of the word a lady, was waiting for a streetcar in downtown Oklahoma City. To her complete, astonished dismay a young man, his denims tucked into his boot tops, stopped before her, removed his ten-gallon Stetson, and bowed politely, a total stranger.

"Ma'am," he enquired, "are you married?" and before she

could rally an answer continued, "I've got a right nice place proved up over north of El Reno, with a two-room house and a dug well, and I saw you standing there and thought to myself, 'Now that'd be something pretty to come home to of an evening.'"

"Sir," said the young lady with generations of Lees and Carrolls behind her, stiffening her already erect spine, "I am engaged." At which point the streetcar arrived and saved them both further embarrassment. Sydney was not reassured by her brother's insistence that the proposal was indeed a compliment.

Sydney returned to Chicago and her fiancé with dispatch, and her daughter still wonders what it would have been like to have been born on a proved-up claim north of El Reno instead of in a North Shore suburb.

Not all proposals were so firmly rejected. Many a match that began as a marriage of convenience "because a man needs a woman around the house and a woman needs someone to look after her," has endured even unto seventy years, with both parties happy and devoted.

Transportation again moved to the fore. There were not only trolley-driven streetcars, there were "interurbans" which ran out of Oklahoma City to Guthrie, Norman and El Reno or between Shawnee and Tecumseh from about 1900 to 1942. Fares were moderate—fifty cents for a round trip, usually. A trip on an interurban was a day's outing for a whole family, with a picnic at the "turn-around" before starting back.

Automobiles appeared. They scared the horses and frightened the livestock, but they had come to stay and Oklahoma has moved on wheels ever since.

Again we have been hopscotching in time and space. In

1904, Oklahoma was not yet a state, although signs and portents of statehood had filled the air since 1890. Not surprisingly, they began in Indian Territory, where people were relatively settled and prosperous, but rapidly spread westward, and soon Oklahoma Territory, too, was asking for statehood.

CHAPTER 7

THE GREAT STATE OF SEQUOYAH

The decisive movement toward statehood began in 1893, when Congress created the Dawes Commission to negotiate with the Five Civilized Tribes for, among other things, individual allotments of lands to the Indians, the establishment of laws to protect the white squatters and to create schools for the white children. The leaders of the Five Civilized Tribes had intermarried with white settlers and occupied as much land as individuals as they could develop through their own efforts or those of tenant farmers for most of the nineteenth century. The other Indians and white settlers survived, partly on the portions doled out to them by the landlords and partly on land they occupied by squatting.

Grover Cleveland, who was President at the time, was not a man to hurry about anything, least of all anything pertaining to Indians. The first of a long series of investigations, task forces, hearings and tribal meetings began. Heretofore, investigators and investigations had glided over the state. They had been abundant, and prolific with reports, but more concerned with the Indians of the northern states than with those who had been conveniently deposited in the back drawer of Oklahoma.

From the time of the Dawes Commission on, the investigative procession through Oklahoma was endless. The status of the Indians in eastern Oklahoma was complicated and fluctuating. On paper all tribes were separate nations, and had been bound to the United States Government by treaties. In 1870, the treaties, which had assured the Indians' autonomy, had been repealed by a blanket bill passed by both houses of Congress. Technically, the treaties were done away with; factually, treaties continued to be made with tribe after tribe. The Five Civilized Tribes were an exception to this bill. They retained their status as independent nations until early 1900.

"Treaty rights" became and have remained the rallying call of all Indians ever since, as "states' rights" had been the rallying call of the South in the Civil War and are now. Under the treaties, the federal government had assumed responsibility for education, health, welfare, law enforcement and roads as these were required or requested. Without the treaties the federal government continued to supply the same services although it was not legally bound to do so. No wonder the Indians—and everybody else—were and remain confused. In 1960, Silas Woods, a Choctaw, asked to distinguish between tribal and governmental functions, produced and read the Preamble to the United States Constitution and the Bill of Rights.

"These are our guarantees," declared Mr. Woods, drawing his granddaddy's Confederate officer's overcoat more closely about him. There must be answers somewhere, but nobody has been able to find them. Mr. Woods with that single sweeping gesture had annihilated the elaborately constructed Choctaw constitution and codified laws, the state's constitution and its code of laws, and had stood forth in his own right—a man and a Choctaw who understood just one thing: He was a citizen of the United States.

On March 28, 1898, the man who was to become to many citizens of the state "Mr. Oklahoma" personified appeared in the Chickasaw capital of Tishomingo to open a law office. William Henry Murray had been born in a one-room, slab-sided shanty near the town of Toadsuck, Texas.

Murray had come up the hard way. He had chopped and picked cotton from the time he was big enough to handle a hoe or drag a tow sack down the rows. He had gone hungry— not only for food, but for learning. Somehow he struggled through College Hill Institution at Springtown, Texas; "small potatoes and a few in a hill," said the president of the institution, when he first saw the prospective student, but Murray stuck it out. He still chopped cotton in the spring and picked it in the fall, which somewhat delayed his education, but what with those jobs, waiting tables in the college dormitory, running errands for anybody who needed an errand run and "reading law" as an apprentice deep into the nights, he made it through.

Before Murray was finally admitted to the Texas bar, he had taught school, been a newspaper reporter in Corsicana, Navarro County, Texas, and earned a well-deserved reputation as a debater in all northeast Texas, no small accomplishment in itself. When the Indian nations opened up for white business and professional men, Murray saw his opportunity, and took it.

Murray was a contentious visionary, a man driven by ambition that would never let him rest. He hung out his shingle, and, preceded by his debating reputation, the young dandy, in top hat and tails, soared into the courtroom in Tishomingo and mowed down his opponents.

It was not only his legal opponents that Murray mowed down. He chose to fall in love with Mary Alice Hearral, niece of the governor of the Chickasaw Nation, Douglas H. Johnston. The upper class of the Chickasaws did not often associate with the townspeople of Tishomingo, but Murray was socially and politically ambitious, and—no fool, but seeing no barriers to acceptance—rushed in where others feared to tread.

Mary Alice was a student at the Chickasaw National Seminary for Young Ladies, later known as Bloomfield Academy, and now as Carter Academy, at Ardmore, when they met at her uncle's home. She was an acknowledged beauty, witty, and accomplished, and played the piano, of course. Later she became a teacher at the academy. Meanwhile, Murray had become a law partner of Governor Johnston.

This put his proposal of marriage on a dignified and worthy basis, and she accepted. The newlywed William Murrays settled down on a farm just outside Tishomingo, where William Murray lay in a hammock slung between two trees and studied his cases and dictated his briefs outdoors when the weather permitted.

It is not our intention to write a biography of Alfalfa Bill Murray—he was the first in the United States to advocate large-scale planting of that legume—although the temptation is great. For the moment our concern is what the Sequoyah Convention in 1902, assembled when it was finally evident that statehood was inevitable and that the Indian nations as such would disappear.

The Convention was called by Governor Pleasant Porter, of the Creeks, and its first meeting was held in Muskogee, in the Creek Nation (it did not seem tactful to select one national capital over the other four). Instead, the city where the Union Agency of the Five Civilized Tribes was located was chosen.

Porter presided and appointed a committee, of which Murray was chairman, to study national and state constitutions generally. Murray afterward said that between 1902 and 1905 he read not only the constitutions of the forty-five states already admitted to the Union, but those of every other nation except England, which had never bothered to write its constitution down.

Murray's considered conclusion was that there were too many loopholes in constitutions generally, and he set out to construct one that would be foolproof. The constitution of the State of Sequoyah was the longest on record, and Murray believed it provided for every possible contingency. It even included licensing laws for automobiles. Not even Murray could then envision supersonic transport and the woes of furious houseowners whose dwellings lay within landing patterns. But it was a mighty constitution, built, like the Deacon's *One Hoss Shay*, never to break down and never to be amended.

The premise was that the State of Sequoyah would comprise the area east of the Cross Timbers, then known as Indian Territory. All five tribal constitutions were considered, and the best part of each was selected. All five tribes outlawed the sale, possession or consumption of alcoholic beverages, and that provision—or prohibition—went into the constitution, with a difference. Formerly the law had applied only to Indians. Now it applied equally to all citizens of the eastern state. Baptists and bootleggers alike cheered for prohibition; the former because they earnestly believed it would bring people closer to God; the latter because it would keep them in business. The incongruous alliance still continues.

It was evident that the State of Sequoyah would be Democratic. Most of the citizens-to-be of western Oklahoma, coming from the northern Middle Western states, were Republicans. It was decided in the United States Congress that the creation of two states would disturb the balance of the Republican power, and the State of Sequoyah was refused, and told to join with its western neighbor as one state.

Here again Alfalfa Bill Murray took the lead. The Constitutional Convention met in 1906 in Guthrie, designated as the territorial capital, with Fritz Franz as territorial governor. The representatives of Indian Territory were practically the same men who had made up the Sequoyah Convention, with Murray again as one of the group who represented the Chickasaws.

Days of wrangling followed over what to call the new state if they ever got it. Finally the Reverend Allan Wright, a leading Choctaw, tactfully suggested combining two Muskhogean words, Okla—meaning red—and Homa—meaning man—and Oklahoma, Home of the Red Man, became the official name of the new state.

The easterners were all adroit and accomplished politicians, far more so than their counterparts from the western side of the state. Delicately, gently, they maneuvered until they made the point that since the State of Sequoyah already had a constitution, there was no need to write another. Just ratify the one already in existence, and go on from there. Oh, a few minor changes could be made, of course, but not in the prohibition clause. On that the eastern tribes stood firm, much to the disappointment of the thriving liquor dealers and saloonkeepers in the west, and to the corresponding rejoicing of the Baptists and the bootleggers.

And once again a constitution had been enacted that could NEVER be amended. It was foolproof. And it was still the longest on record and absolutely guaranteed to put the most determined and insomniac reader to sleep in a matter of minutes. As of 1973, the original constitution of the state of Oklahoma is about to be scrapped and a new one written—the amendments have got out of hand. The original constitution contained, buried in the morass of verbiage, a "grandfather clause"—one's grandfather had to have been a voter before one could vote oneself. This was an inconvenience to those of us whose parents and grandparents were born in other countries. Naturalization papers for at least two generations had to be produced before a voter could register. Also a literacy test was required. This section of the state constitution was nullified by the United States Supreme Court because it exempted certain persons from the test and was an abridgement of the right to vote on account of race, color, or previous conditions of servitude, which was contrary to the United States Constitution.

Segregated schools and school districts were set up for whites and Negroes, though someone managed to stop Murray from imposing the usual Texas restriction which would have created a third series of schools for persons of "Spanish American or Mexican descent." The state could barely maintain one series of schools adequately, and "separate but equal" schooling for Negroes was actually out of the question. The schools were separate but by no means equal.

Negroes had already been denied lands in some of the openings, on the grounds that claims could be taken up only by white persons. One or two Negroes had the courage and determination to fight this clause and to come out with lands, as one or two "buffalo soldier" veterans had insisted on their pension rights, but few were financially able to win.

These matters may have been seen in one light by Murray and his colleagues, but they show in an entirely different way today. Eastern Oklahoma was and remains stubbornly "southern," but it was on the outskirts of central and western Oklahoma towns that signs appeared reading, "Nigger, don't let the sun go down on you here." There are few integrated neighborhoods in Oklahoma cities today, and those could be said to be economically segregated.

School and college lands were set aside under the Constitution, including, after much wrangling, a segregated "university" for Negroes at Langston. Trained Negroes were hard to find as instructors, white teachers at the college level shied away from teaching in a "nigger school," and for many years the university languished at a level slightly lower than junior college. The struggle to maintain it continues, although teaching and basketball standards have improved, and a few white students have been admitted.

Negroes now attend all state-supported institutions of higher learning in Oklahoma, and the bars are also down at public and private schools, elementary, secondary and college level. The process of integration has been relatively painless. A few harsh names may have been called, but no blood has been shed.

CHAPTER 8

FLING OUT THE BANNER—
ALL FORTY-SIX STARS

Probably nothing is duller to some people than political history except military history, and the two often overlap to an alarming degree. The great State of Sequoyah had come and gone; two territories had been brought to the point of agreeing on a single name and a single constitution, and now there arose the question of locating the state capital.

Muskogee would have been the capital of the State of Sequoyah, and many of that state's supporters held out for it to become the capital of Oklahoma. It had good transportation facilities, both by rail and water; it had long been a settled and established town—really a city—and a federal court had been established there.

The capital of Oklahoma Territory was Guthrie. It had good rail access, but no waterways. The Cimarron River, on which Guthrie was located, was not and never had been a navigable stream. Nothing ever had or ever would control that river, whose name in Spanish meant "wild" or "uncontrollable."

We're going to succumb to temptation and tell here another version of how the river got its name. According to legend, two cowboys camped on its bank one night. There was little dry wood available, the cook fire was slow in starting, they were hungry and tired and impatient for a cup of coffee. At last one man leaped to his feet and kicked the coffeepot into the river, yelling,

"Simmer on, Goddamn you, simmer on!" And so was the river named.

Guthrie itself, a railhead for the Rock Island and Santa Fe railroads, a stock shipping point, and fairly near the new oil fields that were beginning to open up, had a rough and ready reputation. It also had mineral springs, a bathhouse, a large and elegant hotel, the Ione, which was famous for its food, and plenty to offer in competition with Muskogee, although the prohibition clause in the state constitution had damaged one of its major industries.

Oklahoma City, thirty miles south of Guthrie, and Tulsa, fifty miles west of Muskogee, also advanced their claims for the glory of becoming the state's first capital. In spite of all arguments, however, Guthrie, the territorial capital, became the first capital city of Oklahoma.

On November 16, 1907, Mr. Oklahoma Territory, in cowboy boots and ten-gallon Stetson hat, married Miss Indian Territory, a Choctaw clad in an anything-but-appropriate beaded buckskin Cheyenne dress, on the steps of the Logan County Courthouse. The exact wording of the nuptial ceremony seems to have been lost. Charles Haskell was sworn in as governor of the state. He was already territorial governor. The state of Oklahoma formally came into existence. The inaugural ball was held in the Ione Hotel, and the courthouse became the first state capitol.

Oklahoma City was still in a pout, and it is characteristic of Oklahoma City that it did something about it. Legend has it that with the blessing of the governor, who had chosen it over Guthrie as his home town, a contingent of legislators and supporters descended on Guthrie, removed the state seal and what records there were of the administration (they filled, said one participant, a single filing cabinet), and removed the state government to Oklahoma City. Driving in the dark of night over back roads—and all roads were "back" by eastern standards—a Model-T Ford, carrying the governor, the papers and the seal, was said to have reached Oklahoma City before dawn. All hands removed the loot to the Lee-Huckins Hotel, at the southeast corner of Main and Broadway, which had a locked safe, and proceeded to celebrate the dawn of the new day. "If we win we'll celebrate; if we lose; we'll dissipate," had been Max Cunningham's motto since boyhood. They celebrated. Guthrie complained, but it was too late for action.

The Victorian-Gothic object which was to become Oklahoma County's first courthouse was still building. Its yellow brick walls were up but the interior was incomplete, and it could not be used as a capitol pro tem. The hotel became the state capitol building for the next two years. After all, it was only a block from the City Hall, which had been established above a saloon—until the saloon was closed by the prohibition clause. The old City Hall building succumbed to urban renewal in February 1971, and the Huckins in July of the same year.

And now began a hassle over where the official state capitol building should be located. Like the state, Oklahoma City was divided into two parts, this time by the Canadian River. The settlement south of the river, where the stockyards were, called itself in lordly fashion Capitol Hill, blandly ignoring the fact that it was low lying and subject to flooding when the Canadian, like the Cimarron, felt temperamental.

Northward the land rose, and the railroad stations were located. The Rock Island station was only a block from the Lee-Huckins Hotel, two blocks north of the City Hall. The Katy Railroad station (Missouri, Kansas and Texas usually abbreviated to M.K.T.) was two blocks east, and the Santa Fe three blocks south of the Rock Island. The hotel provided an eligible central location, but it could not provide it forever because the city was growing up around it. Two survey parties, one starting from Capitol Hill and one from the northern city limits at Tenth Street, had just failed to meet, providing a jog where north-south streets crossed Grand Avenue. This jog could be rationalized—and was—by the statement that it was a section line, and that section lines always "took a bend at a corner."

To everyone's surprise, and to the horror of many, the location finally selected was "clear out in the boondocks, outside the city limits." A mile east of the Santa Fe tracks, at the junction of Twenty-third Street and Lincoln Boulevard. Both streets were still on the drawing boards at that time, but by the time the question of architecture was settled, they had been surveyed and partially paved, and the land included in the Oklahoma City limits.

The contract for the building went to the architectural firm of Layton, Hicks, and Forsyth, with the youngest partner, George Forsyth, entrusted with the design of the structure. Buildings and grounds supervisor C. L. Smith was appointed to work with Mr. Forsyth. Max Cunningham, by this time state highway engineer, was designated to lay out approaches to the building.

This was a tight little British Empire which joined hands against the onslaughts of Kansas and Texas. Forsyth had recently come from Edinburgh. Cunningham and Smith were first-generation Americans; one of English and one of Irish descent. Whatever the historical differences between the lands of their heritage might have been, on one point the three were in complete agreement: THERE SHOULD BE NO DOME ON THIS STATE CAPITOL. They had seen most of those already in existence, and "a hell of a lot of courthouses," and they had decided individually and collectively that domes were a blot on the landscape.

Forsyth designed a building whose Greek purity of design is truly classic. Just to be on the safe side, he designed it so that a dome which looked presentable from north and south would be an eyesore for viewers from east and west. Together, he and Cunningham worked out structural stressess and weight-bearing beams which would not support a dome physically. Every state legislature that has met since the building opened in 1916 has passed a bill "to dome up the capitol," and then got out the blueprints—to go down in defeat.

The old county courthouse disappeared under the onslaught of WPA construction in the 1930s. Urban renewal has torn down the first City Hall, and the Huckins (as it became) has been dynamited to make way for a parking lot. But the capitol, built of Henryetta granite and faced inside with other native stones, remains, somewhat incongruous among the modern state office buildings which surround it, but a monument to purity, dignity—and the stubbornness of three men.

The capitol building faced south, and from the plaza before it rose a two-story flight of marble stairs—Oklahoma marble, it need hardly be said. Inside the building the flight continued upward another two floors, to the fourth-floor rotunda from which the two legislative chambers opened.

In order to do justice to this stately main entry, Smith and Cunningham planned an avenue approach a mile long, stretching from Thirteenth Street on the south to Twenty-first on the north, where the street broadened into the plaza. The avenue was divided by a parkway, and a sunken rose garden was designed, with fountains and walkways, to adorn the park.

By one of those merciless acts of fate, the Depression of the 1930s and the discovery of oil under and around the capitol coincided. The approach is now adorned by a mile-long stretch of far-from-sunken oil wells, and busily pumping "grasshoppers" surround the icebox modern state office buildings that have been built north and south of the original structure. Only the Historical Society Building, to the south and east, carries out the Greek architecture of the capitol proper.

Attempts to adorn the rotunda have been equally conflicting. From it two wings stretch southward on the east and west sides of the main staircase. An artist was imported from Paris—France, not Texas—to do a mural at the end of each wing: one depicting Oklahoma mourning the loss of citizens in World War I, the other, the doughboy returning in glory to the outstretched arms of his state.

Four niches were built around the rotunda proper, and it was planned originally that they would contain life-size statues of illustrious Oklahomans, with each wing lined with busts of the slightly less illustrious. So far as we know, none of the statues ever got off the drawing board, let alone into the capitol.

In the 1950s, Governor Howard Edmondson, with the blessing of the state legislature, commissioned Charles Banks Wilson, of Miami, Oklahoma, an artist of great talent and ability, to paint a portrait of a distinguished Oklahoman in the background of each niche. By that time, Oklahoma had produced enough citizens of distinction for four subjects to be available: Sequoyah, the Cherokee, who, illiterate in English, a language he could not even speak, alone in history invented a syllabic system for writing his own language; Jim Thorpe, Sauk and Fox, "the one-man Olympic team," Governor and later United States Senator Robert S. Kerr, who was responsible for the development of commercially feasible waterways; and, naturally, Will Rogers, entertainer, newspaper columnist and "ambassador to the world."

Wilson spent almost seven years on the portraits, working on each one singly, studying and researching his subjects with a diligence many historians might envy, and producing portraits of living men, ready to step from the wall and speak to the observer. He, of all artists who at one time or another have decorated public buildings in Oklahoma, grasped the beauty of the surrounding country and the dignity of the men he portrayed. When his work was finished, asked what was the hardest part of it, Wilson quietly replied,

"Jim Thorpe's knee muscles. It was just like painting a bag of beans, they were so relaxed and so knit together." These portraits are not only monuments to the men they portray, but to the man who portrayed them.

CHAPTER 9

AND THEN CAME OIL

Oklahoma City may be the capital of the state, but Tulsa, ninety miles to the east on the other side of the Cross Timbers, is the oil capital of the world, and any Tulsan will be glad and proud to tell you so.

The first producing oil well was brought in by the Choctaw Oil and Refining Company at the Faucett Ranch on Clear Boggy Creek in the northwest corner of Atoka County in 1887. Bartlesville's Nellie Johnson No. 1 is usually considered the state's first "producing" well because it had more publicity, but it was brought in in 1897.

Oil activity spread across the state, and the drilling locations are almost a roster of the state's principal cities: Bartlesville, Tulsa, Enid, Seminole, Wewoka, Muskogee and Oklahoma City. The list actually is almost endless.

In the beginning, the oil game was a rough and rugged one, and it was sometimes impossible to identify the players as individuals. Oil was where you found it, and if there was no town nearby, the next best thing was to bring in a well, start it pumping—if you could—and worry about building a city later.

Oil geology was only beginning then, as a serious field of research, and some of the first oil geologists who worked in Oklahoma were imported. One of them, Rudolph Brauchli (who recently returned to Muri, Switzerland), brought his wife and daughter with him to what was in process of becoming the present city of Seminole, and their son was born there, in the second story of a wooden building, over an illegal saloon. Susan Brauchli was a woman of background and education, a talented musician, and a speaker of French, German, Italian and Romanisch. Many years later she confessed that she first learned English from that spoken on the lower floor, beneath her apartment, and that her husband had to spend an hour a night cleaning up her vocabulary.

For the oil fields had "a slanguage," as E. G. "Ty" Dahlgren, another early-day geologist and consultant, calls it, all their own. Dahlgren's background was Swedish, but he had been born and educated in Wisconsin.

When we were first doing research for this book, Mr. Dahlgren suggested that we ask a student, who had worked as an oil field roustabout, to write a term paper defining S.O.B. ("son of a bitch"). Mr. Dahlgren was referring to the escape guy wire running from the top of the rig to the ground, down which a man caught on the crown block when a well blew in could slide to safety. The student produced nine papers in eighteen weeks, each with a different definition of the term, but none of them referring to the escape guy. In desperation we appealed to Mr. Dahlgren for a simile—it began to seem as if anything at all in an oil field could be called an S.O.B. Mr. Dahlgren suggested "Geronimo," the paratroopers' yell, which men returning from World War II had brought to the oil fields with them. This produced the desired definition of a guy wire, and the bewildered, innocent inquiry from the student, "Why didn't you say that first? I thought it was kind of funny for ladies to be so interested in the other words." The only possible answer was that we weren't ladies, we were anthropologists, but we refrained.

Nobody ever knew where the mud came from, but pictures of early oil towns always show them as knee-deep in mud. Susan Brauchli, that model of ladylike dress and deportment, put aside her Paris gowns in favor of laced knee boots and breeches like those her husband wore, so that she might cross the Seminole streets without ruining her wardrobe piecemeal. It is hard today, watching the elegant visiting Mrs. Brauchli lay aside her mink stole at a symphony concert, to remember that she once dressed and swore like a man—profanity being the only English she knew. It is equally hard to visualize the white-haired, dignified Dr. Brauchli, presiding over a meeting of the symphony board, as the hardhanded driver of the mule team he used when his Model-T Ford could go no farther toward a well. Oklahomans, wherever they were born and educated, remain flexible.

People like Dr. and Mrs. Brauchli brought their backgrounds with them, whether from Europe or from the eastern United States, and their persistence in maintaining certain standards of taste in music, painting, home decoration and the like did much to change rugged frontier towns into surprising outposts of good music, ballet and other arts.

The oil world was a young world. Only young men could stand the physical work and the physical hardships entailed in exploration, drilling, spudding in and capping the wells. The wife of an oil geologist, declining a dinner invitation for her husband, will still say, quite spontaneously, "I'm so sorry; he's sitting up with a sick well and can't get away tonight."

Only young women had the courage and endurance to follow their men to the fields, whether as wives or camp followers. And the oil towns were lively places. Much of the old "hitting town on a Saturday night" spirit of Remington's cowmen revived in the roustabouts and deckhands who took their turns on the "towers" (tours of duty) of twelve and sometimes twenty-four hours' duration.

Many of the first oil wells were "wildcatters," located by independent, get-rich-quick types. The seismograph had not yet been invented. You located a well by the seat of your pants, looking at the shape of the surrounding landscape while sitting on a hill. A depression between two rolling mounds of earth meant a depression in the strata below; hence, a pool of oil *might* have collected there. The best thing to do was to bring up a steam-powered drill and dig in. Abandoned steam boilers still dot the older fields, mute victims of the diesel age.

Sometimes the well was shallow, and the oil lay near the surface of the ground, even seeping through occasionally. A drill might penetrate the pool unexpectedly, sending the black stream streaking up the sky, and making the escape wire a necessity for the man directing operations from the crown block, which was really an outsized pulley. A gusher was not a desirable well. It wasted a lot of oil before it could be capped in and brought under control, and the oil that slicked over the ground rendered it unfit for planting or grazing for years, if not forever.

Nobody who has not seen the plume of oil rise from the earth—black to pale golden brown, depending on the purity of the oil—can quite imagine the excitement of "watching a wild one blow in." Nor until one has seen an oil gusher catch fire, or a gas well blow in with a flare of white and red, can one know what terror is. Residents in the vicinity, sometimes for a ten-mile circuit, must be evacuated until the torch is brought under control. The rig lies on the ground, a twisted blackened metal skeleton, instead of standing tall and straight, a man-made tree.

Special techniques have had to be developed to deal with oil-well fires. First, in the early days of the fields, drillers hurried to dig an offset, a hole first parallel to, then directed into the inferno. Dynamite or nitroglycerin detonated in the offset *might* stop the flame at its source. At present, trained fire-fighting crews in asbestos suits work directly over the hole and drop the explosive without wasting time in offset drilling. These are the heroes of the oil fields—the men revered by all other oil workers.

The first men to finance oil-well drilling were not scientists. Few of them had more than a grade-school education, if that. They were born gamblers, as exemplified by Thomas Gilcrease of Tulsa. Thomas Gilcrease, like many other men who gained prominence in Oklahoma, grew bored with country school teaching, dabbled in politics and finally backed an associate with a drill rig.

Gilcrease was an enrolled Creek Indian, and because of his persuasiveness a Creek couple named Glenn allowed him to drill on their land near Seminole. What came up was the great Glenn Pool, probably the most famous of such discoveries.

The Glenn Pool was relatively shallow, and the oil was so abundant that rigs were set within forty feet of one another. It was not until many years later that the Federal Oil and Gas Commission stepped in to control the spacing of wells, the number of hours each well might be pumped each month ("the pro-ratas" said the oil men, who hated them) and put an end to the wild scramble to get as much out of the ground as it would yield.

For a time it seemed that every man was his own company. Some joined forces with other drillers; then drew back and worked as "independents"; then amalgamated their interests with a second partner's. Finally, eastern money began to back the fields, and at present most of the oil in Oklahoma is controlled, with the blessing of the Federal Corporation Commission, through such international firms as Sun, Gulf, Conoco, Texaco and Chevron-Humble. Quotas are set, pro-ratas established, and the oil world moves on: offshore and across the seas, with its headquarters in low-taxed Texas.

At this point a distinction, which is also a clear-cut difference, must be made between a *product* and an *industry*. Oil production itself is not now a major Oklahoma occupation. It consumes the time and attention of relatively few persons, all of them specialists in their fields. It is the oil industry which is of major importance in Oklahoma, with its processing, refining, catalytic (or "crack") plants, its pipelines and shooting wars between international oil companies and the landowners into whose soil they wish to bulldoze and lay pipes, that gives the state its place as an oil state. Oil production itself is not negligible, but it is far less important than in other regions.

The offshore drilling in California, Louisiana, and southern Florida has produced oil in far greater quantities, and with far more headaches for ecologists, than in Oklahoma. At least everyone connected with the oil industry in Oklahoma can blithely agree that the soil from which they take the oil was no damn good to anyone in the first place.

Seminole, capital of Seminole County, had its rough and ready heyday, but did not really compare with the ructions that went on in Spindletop, Burke-Burnett, and Borger, Texas, or with those of the Louisiana Cajun country or even the Pennsylvania oil fields in the days of their early openings. Procurers and prostitutes followed the oil fields as they had the military, and no one place can assert a claim for roughness superior to any other. Procurers and prostitutes supplied immediate biological needs, wherever they were, as did "cafes" and "rooming houses," where men slept one tower, or shift, to a bed the clock around.

Without indulging in statistics—they are, after all, on record with the Interstate Commerce Commission and the various state oil commissions involved—we can safely say that the oil *industry* has been of great importance in Oklahoma, while oil production has played second or third fiddle to that of other states. E. W. Marland, M.F.H., did not lead the Osage Hills fox hounds baying across the prairies in pursuit of coyotes, which his melton-pink hunt meet innocently attempted to run down, no foxes being available, on the strength of his producing wells. It was on the strength of his refining and processing plants, and, as he dolefully remarked, "My name disappeared and Conoco was put in its place. The old Marland Oil Company was a thing of the past. The house of Morgan had merged it out of existence." Such is the history of many an independent oil producer. Millionaires became paupers overnight as the big companies moved in and took over the really paying part of the business.

Oil has created, with the able assistance of the major European nations, empires in Kuwait and Saudi Arabia. These are even more wild and woolly than Oklahoma was at its worst. The same thing is happening around the globe.

"Oil is where you find it," and until the seat of his pants wears out someone, somewhere, will be sitting on the slope of one anticline after another, and hoping—and waiting—

The primary industry of Oklahoma, as we have already said, is the production of cattle. Not only mature feeder stock but the calf crops bring more money into the state than oil ever has or will. This is especially true since Oklahoma oil-processing taxes have gone up and Texas oil-processing taxes have gone down. Major oil companies are departing Tulsa for Houston with depressing regularity.

Yes, the cow and calf crops, which can be processed elsewhere with no expensive investments, represent the largest return per capita to the grazers and growers. In good years the cattle can be pastured on native grasses and "harvest the hay on the hoof." In bad years the cutting and baling of the surplus hay and alfalfa of the good years will sustain them. Cattle have been shipped from faraway Australia (by air, naturally, so they would not lose weight enroute) to Oklahoma grasslands for fattening.

Nor is the bull crop to be despised. Dr. Allen J. Stanley, geneticist and former professor of physiology at the Oklahoma University School of Medicine, was "imported" by the Charolais Cattle Breeders' Association of Dordogne, France, to apply his expert knowledge of breeding to sterile Charolais bulls. He did so successfully and even introduced the breed into the southwestern states, where everybody expected it to curl up and die, with equal success. Charolais crossed with Indian Brahmas are some of the finest meat-producing animals to be found in the world.

Wheat and cotton, which once were major Oklahoman crops, are now, God be thanked, on their way out. They have exhausted the soil, which must be enriched by plantings of nitrogen-rich native grasses and alfalfa. They are still productive crops in some areas, but are lagging more and more.

What has all this to do with oil? Nothing—and everything. Oil earned an undeserved name for the state, on the basis of lack of definition. There are other crops such as pecans and peanuts which take over abandoned oil fields and enrich, not deplete the soil, and are becoming per capita cash crops of major importance. We shall never see the end of oil production, but we can begin to put it in its proper relative position.

With the development of atomic and nuclear energy, it may even be hoped that the internal combustion engine and its attendant pollution and pollutants will disappear from the face of the earth, and it will no longer be necessary to undermine the structure of said earth to extract what was once known as "black gold."

But it was swell while it lasted! Men like Thomas Gilcrease, Ernest Marland, a Ponca City politician who eventually became governor, or the Phillips brothers, Frank, Lee and Waite, who had abandoned their Bartlesville barber shop for wildcatting, went to bed relatively poor, all they had sunk in one hopeful hole in the ground, and woke up millionaires. They had money they hadn't folded; more money than they could count; more money, actually, then they knew what to do with.

Marland, with more formal education than the others, was the first to take a trip abroad before World War I. He returned to build a thirty-room house, in Mediterranean style, surrounded by gardens. His gardens were tended by gardeners imported from Japan. He planned a museum and a heroic statue of a pioneer woman, to be his gift to Ponca City and a tribute to his wife.

About that time Mrs. Marland took umbrage at some unknown cause, divorced her husband and left Oklahoma forever.

Mr. Marland married his wife's niece, whose guardian he had been. The whole matter was a little too much even for the men of the oil fields, and the statue was dedicated as a tribute to Mr. Marland's mother.

Twelve sculptors were invited to submit scale models of a thirty-foot figure. All were men and women of great skill and knowledge, but each had his or her own idea what a pioneer woman must look like, and none of them came to Oklahoma seeking a model in the flesh. The results ranged from the recognizable to the barely so. The contract eventually went to Bryant Baker, a New Yorker, who built the mold and made the cast for the finished statue in a Brooklyn waterfront warehouse—the only place he could find that was big enough. It was shipped to Oklahoma by rail.

On a spring morning in 1922, everybody who could get there assembled in Ponca City at the foot of the statue, before the Marland mansion on land which later became a city park, to hear Will Rogers dedicate it. The only detail of his dedicatory address remembered by one listener is the observation, "The pioneer woman could take long swingin' steps like this gal, all right, but I wonder how the lady manages with her corsets when she gets dressed up." Beside the pioneer mother, and looking up at her while he holds her right hand, is her son. Against her heart, under her left arm, she clasps a Bible. It is a beautiful and dramatic sight with which time has dealt kindly, for the bronze has an even patination that adds to its loveliness.

All twelve models submitted in the contest had toured the state, and the people had voted on the one to be commissioned. The decision was not Marland's own. Once the vote was in and counted, the models were stored away in the basement of the mansion. There, years later, after Marland's death, they were discovered by the director of Frank Phillips' Woolaroc (Woods, Lakes, Rocks) Museum, William "Pat" Patterson, and "captured" for the Phillips' collection at Bartlesville.

And that brings us to the Phillips brothers again. Lee stayed home and minded the oil office, running the business as long as the brothers operated as a team. But Frank and Waite traveled. They not only traveled, they collected. At one time it was said at museum meetings that Frank Phillips had to sit on the board of the museum association because the only way to keep other collections safe was to have him at the head table, with everybody watching him.

Frank Phillips' Woolaroc Museum and ranch are among the sights of Oklahoma that, once seen, can never be forgotten. South of Bartlesville, in north-central Oklahoma, are one hundred sixty acres of woodland, with bulldozed lakes, a magnificent ranch house and all the necessary outbuildings, and a native stone museum that, when it was built, was the last, ultimate word in museum construction. This was Phillips' bequest to the people of Oklahoma.

The land was stocked with grazing animals of every kind: native buffalo, Scotch Highland cattle, Sicilian donkeys, caribou, every kind of deer or antelope that could stand the Oklahoma climate—or, as Will Rogers said, "We don't have climate. We have weather"—was included. The ponds were stocked with fish, and picnic tables and benches erected under the shade trees. A "Tombstone Graveyard" for legendary bad men was designed for a damp, soggy hollow on the drive up to the ranch house; the skulls of slaughtered animals were nailed to the trees, and everything possible was done to create a Spook Hollow. Cigar-store Indians, too numerous for any museum to house, were dotted over the landscape, and brightly repainted each spring. The grounds were a sight to behold.

But the museum! Patterson himself once termed it "Aunt Martha's attic," but philosophically added that Mr. Phillips liked it that way. As much as possible, the museum's motif was Indian. Navaho rugs hung against the walls, and paintings of Indian subjects, from calendar art up and down, hung against the rugs. In a central case was a cut-away model of a Crow tipi, and when a visitor pushed the button, Indian music (recorded before the day of tape recorders) drummed over the room, while the foot-high occupants of the tipi whirled in a wild war dance. In another central case were models of the artifacts from the great Spiro mound in Leflore County, in eastern Oklahoma. Phillips had helped to finance the excavation and Patterson had worked on the site as an undergraduate student, so it was at Spiro that their trails first crossed.

Daylight never enters the Woolaroc Museum; fresh air never blows through it. All light and ventilation are artificially controlled. It was the first such museum built in Oklahoma, and an architectural triumph, complete to photographic dark rooms, display construction rooms and offices. Patterson, that irrepressible Irishman, stood for the weight of the ages as long as he could; then supplied each case with a series of cartoon drawings of the artifacts as they were used.

Downstairs, was the "personal" collection of Mr. and Mrs. Phillips, including the clothing given them when they were adopted as members of the Osage tribe, displayed on life-size figures. Here again, although not until after Mr. Phillips' death, Patterson could not resist the lighter touch, and he seated the two figures in chairs made from the horns of longhorn steers. "I figured they oughta be tired after all those years standing up," he observed, adding, "Anyway, we had the chairs around and I couldn't see that they added much anywhere else."

Patterson is not a formally trained museum man. He holds a degree in anthropology from the University of Oklahoma and had done some work in the university museum when Mr. Phillips decided to employ him. Like Aunt Martha's attic, Patterson suited Mr. Phillips—suited him so well, in fact, that when Phillips died the one condition of his bequest of the museum to the city of Bartlesville was that Patterson be retained as permanent director. He retired in 1970, at his own decision, still a relatively young man.

An untrained director might suit Frank Phillips and be at home on the ranch, but would not do for his brother Waite. When Waite decided to convert his own Mediterranean villa—formal gardens, gold spiggots in the bathrooms, a sunken onyx tub in the floor of his private bath, and Howard Chandler Christy murals of Mrs. Phillips dancing with wreathed garlands in the music room—he looked around for a director who would be worthy to administer this splendor, which he called Philbrook Museum after himself and the creek that flowed through the grounds.

Waite Phillips' choice fell on Eugene Kingman, a New Englander and himself a painter. Kingman had just received one of the first degrees in museum work conferred by Yale University. He had worked during his university summers at Mesa Verde National Park as a museum ranger, and it was there he had met his Denver-born wife. Together they made a team that could be beaten only by war and a board of directors. Kingman entered service in 1942; when he was discharged he went to Omaha's Jocelyn Museum.

Under Kingman's direction, Philbrook Museum in four years, 1938-42, assembled the nucleus of an art collection; cleaned, sorted and displayed a bewildering variety of Indian artifacts; became the permanent home of the Clark Field collection of American Indian baskets and pottery; established the Southwest Art Association, which eventually owned and maintained the building and instituted one of the best educational programs in fine arts in the United States.

The necessity for teaching space conveniently did away with the onyx bathtub and the golden plumbing, but the Christy murals remained for sometime. When Kingman requested leave of absence to go into service, the management of the museum finances was put in the hands of one of Mr. Phillips' business associates, Victor Hurt, and Mr. Hurt handles the purse strings today. Museum directors may come or go; unless they have Mr. Hurt's knowledge and consent they cannot institute programs, or even carry on existing ones. The maintenance of the building is financed from Waite Phillips' gift to the Southwestern Art Association of a downtown office building, the Philtower, and Mr. Hurt managed the office building as well as the museum finances, until the Philtower was sold in the 1960s and the money reinvested.

For years the brothers, Frank and Waite, carried on a lively feud in collecting. Finally, the National Gallery in Washington turned down part of a gift from the great S. H. Kress collection of paintings. Philbrook offered the paintings a permanent home; there was a banquet and a grand installation in a newly constructed gallery built for the collection, and Frank Phillips died soon after. There are those who were unkind enough to say that he died of a broken heart, because his brother had "beat him out" at last.

We have both been so intimately associated with Philbrook—one of us from its very beginning—that it is hard to keep from going on and on about it. The building now is four or five times the original size—and the enlarging has been done without damaging the gardens, which are a delight in themselves. The educational programs have expanded and enlarged, always under competent directorship. An annual show and competition for Indian artists has become one of Philbrook's main events and one of the most respected exhibitions of Indian art anywhere. The late Clark Field, at ninety, and as he admitted, "a little tottery sometimes," took Sunday guided tours through his collection. Mr. Field made as much effort to please and interest a single Boy Scout as he did a large ladies' club. It was worth a trip to Tulsa to hear him in action.

Philbrook in all its loveliness is on the east side of Tulsa. Across town, on the border between Osage and Tulsa counties and in the rolling Osage Hills, stands the place that Thomas Gilcrease chose for his permanent home, and we do mean permanent, for his tomb is one of the features of the grounds. At the crest of the hill is the simple, blocky native stone house which he built when he first struck oil, and extending along the ridge to the north is the Gilcrease Institute, a massive modern structure, which houses his art and Indian collection. The tomb, in addition to Mr. Gilcrease, was intended to house his friend and onetime artist-in-residence, the Pawnee painter Acee Blue Eagle. However, Blue Eagle, a veteran of World War II, is buried in the military cemetery at Fort Gibson.

The Gilcrease museum is no Aunt Martha's attic. It too is closed to daylight and fresh air, and as an additional attraction the temperature is held year round at a steady 70 degrees. Storerooms, photographic dark rooms, all construction rooms are spotless; the collection is magnificently catalogued, and it includes an archive and library on Oklahoma and its Indians which is probably the finest in the state. (Opinions always differ about what is "finest" in such areas.)

However, in his early days, Mr. Gilcrease was what is known as "the pack-rat type of collector." He collected everything that caught his eye and his interest, including Oklahoma's first Miss America, Norma Des Cygnes Smallwood.

As time went on, and Gilcrease traveled and observed other museums, he decided that he, too, would confine his collection to Indian objects and themes. He engaged Martin Wiesendanger, a Swiss-born employee of Knoedler Galleries, New York, and the two went on a buying spree that has seldom been equaled. They ranged from Mexico to Canada and back and forth; purchased from eastern and European galleries and accumulated a wealth of material.

In fact, Mr. Gilcrease became so absorbed in his collecting that he all but neglected the business that supported it. His wife had long since taken their baby daughter, divorced him and moved to California. The collection seemed to be all he had left to live for. Yet the day came when Thomas Gilcrease discovered that he was a millionaire on paper only, and that collecting must cease. He offered the museum building and its collection to the city of Tulsa, specifying only that he retain life tenancy of his home and that he be buried, with Blue Eagle, on its grounds.

The announcement that the Gilcrease Collection had been offered for sale—not to say put up for grabs—started a flurry in the eastern markets. The two largest paintings Thomas Moran had executed in his life, "Lower Falls of the Yellowstone" and "Glory of the Canyon," were included. So were priceless objects of pre-Columbian Mexican art, a part of the omnipresent Spiro Collection (it has been spread over the landscape so widely that even the original site cataloguer is not sure what piece is where, or whether she is looking at a copy or an original), a Thomas Eakins portrait of anthropologist Frank Hamilton Cushing, a holograph letter from Diego Columbus to his father, Christopher, and a vast quantity of contemporary Indian art and artifacts. All were eventually purchased by the city of Tulsa, and remained in the Gilcrease Institute.

The truth is that it has been as hard for us to be objective about the Gilcrease Institute as about Philbrook. We know too much—and too little. We can only say that whether the collections were gathered in rivalry or in a spirit of aesthetic admiration, they are unequaled in their fields.

CHAPTER 10

THE EDIFICE COMPLEX

As the preceding pages have suggested, Oklahomans will not only always be moving, they will always be building. "From tipis to towers," the State Planning Commission says modestly. Not for them the staid, tree-lined streets of white cottages of New England and the smaller Pennsylvania towns. With few exceptions they scorn the white-pillared classic revival houses of ante-bellum southern cities. When Oklahomans build, they want to build BIG. Tree planting and other falderals can come later.

Probably the state's major educational institutions are the most shining examples of this urge to make it bigger and, if not better, definitely different.

The University of Oklahoma, at Norman, started out sedately with a Victorian-Gothic administration building which for some years also served as a classroom building. Two administration buildings in succession burned, to be rebuilt in the same style. Construction of the first building began in 1890, one year after the first land run, while classes were held in a downtown store building until it was completed. For some reason, authorities stuck to Victorian Gothic for the administration building, through thick and thin, and the present building, completed in 1900, is in the same style.

However, the University of Oklahoma rapidly outgrew its first building. A long north and south oval was designed, with the administration building at its south end, and other structures on east and west sides. Some, like the educational and home economics buildings, were severely utilitarian, practical stone blocks. The law and chemistry buildings, facing each other, are faintly (only faintly) architecturally reminiscent of Notre Dame Cathedral.

Another oval was laid out east of the first one; then two more, including the stadium and the field house, south of the other two. The library backed the administration building, and between them a rose garden was laid out.

The gardens are the glory of the University of Oklahoma. Seasonal plantings bloom the year round, and even though the campus has grown so large that mini-buses must be used to transport students between classroom buildings, every available foot of earth is landscaped and planted.

At one time the School of Petroleum Engineering was the largest in the world, and it still attracts students from every country under the sun. The De Golyer Collection of books on the history of science, and particularly Mr. De Golyer's own science, petroleum engineering, is one of the marvels of the campus. So is Frank Phillips' Collection of books on Indians and the history of the West, willed to the university because he was a close friend—who wasn't?—of the late Edward Everett Dale, Ph.D., then head of the Department of History and later emeritus professor.

Town and gown are separated in Norman. In fact, they were meant to be, and town planning called for a separation of at least a mile between campus and business district. Student and faculty housing were at a premium from the beginning, however, and the problems were solved by faculty members who built houses ever nearer the campus, and who rented rooms to students. Now the two merge geographically, but the intellectual division persists to some extent.

At the time one of us was the first woman to take a degree in anthropology at the University of Oklahoma, it was necessary to live in a "girls' rooming house," and take meals with her brothers, in a "boys' boardinghouse" next door. Undergraduate students were forbidden to own automobiles, and if a young woman sat on a young man's lap in a parent's car there must be a cushion between them. Enrollment stood at five thousand, of which four thousand were male. It was heaven!

The town-gown separation in Norman was further increased by the fact that the state institution for the mentally ill was located on the east edge of the community. If you said to another Oklahoman, "I'm going to Norman," the answer invariably was "East side or west side? You have to show improvement to get out on the east." It remains a standing local joke.

In 1942, immediately after Pearl Harbor, land the university owned north and south of the city was leased to the Navy, and the north and south bases came into existence. There are still reminders of the World War II years in the reconditioned barracks which were used to house students after the war; the hutments for housing married students until apartments could be built, and the term "Good Ship Oklahoma," which is sometimes heard. Boys who enlisted in the Navy had not expected to be trained in the middle of the continent. Equally disappointed were the girls who enlisted as Waves, and trained at Oklahoma State University at Stillwater.

Both these universities, Langston University for Negroes, and the many state "normal schools" for teacher training in different areas of the state are land grant colleges; that is, they must be administered by separate Boards of Regents *and* by a Board of Regents for Higher Education; they must offer military and teacher training; and they must meet certain educational standards.

For many years all college level schools were segregated, but in 1949 the bars began to be lowered, first in the graduate school at Norman; later at undergraduate level in all schools. A Negro friend, a graduate in sociology of the University of Chicago, working at the University of Oklahoma on her M.A. degree in the same subject, was asked whether she felt the other students rejected or discriminated against her.

"Sometimes I wish they did," she sighed. "Everybody is so determined to make me feel at home that I can't get a cup of coffee and sit down to study in the cafeteria without having a dozen people rushing up to shake hands and see how I'm doing. I'm glad they're so friendly, of course," she added, "but it's lowering my grade point average."

All colleges and universities in Oklahoma show striking evidence of the edifice complex. Apparently, some attempt at uniformity was made in the beginning, because each one started out with a standard Victorian-Gothic administration building. The one on our own campus, Central State University, at Edmond, called Old North, opened a month before the University of Oklahoma and is the oldest educational building in continuous use in Oklahoma.

From about 1900 on, however, styles began to vary more and more widely. At the moment icebox modern is the campus rage. Pure functionalism, say educators, with no distracting gewgaws. The great exception to this is the Rupel Jones Theatre on the campus at Norman—a gem of the best modern design.

Sometimes it seems as if Oklahoma has been a proving ground for architectural ideas. Frank Lloyd Wright designed the Price Tower, an office building, in Bartlesville, and a home in Tulsa. Like many Frank Lloyd Wright structures, these are aesthetic jewels, but the roofs leak, although that matter is politely ignored by everyone.

Buckminster Fuller frankly experimented with the geodesic dome to be shown at the Moscow World's Fair when he designed the Citizen's National Bank Building in Oklahoma City, 1958, the world's first such structure in anodized aluminum. One of his former classmates, viewing it for the first time, smote his forehead and moaned, "Good old Bucky Fuller and his geodesic domes! I knew he'd do it sometime; he's just that stubborn."

South of the domed bank rises the Citizen's Bank Tower, an office building, and another Fuller-designed anodized aluminum structure. The effect of the two, side by side, is somewhat phallic, but most Oklahomans have nice clean minds and mouths and don't give utterance to such opinions even if they experience them.

Connor and Pojezny committed the Dairy Queen, as Oklahoma City's First Christian Church is known. We went away for a vacation and returned to find the corner at Thirty-sixth Street and Walker decorated with this mammalian structure, which is said to seat five thousand persons, if five thousand want to be seated in the same place at the same time. The minister rises to his pulpit on an elevator, illuminated winter and summer, day and night, by a shaft of light from above. (The minister for whom it was designed had a striking head of red hair, and got the full effect.)

Fortunately, George Forsyth was still alive to design the civic-county complex in downtown Oklahoma City, and his hand rests lovingly on its Grecian purity, a fitting match for the clean lines and dignity of the capitol building. Unfortunately, other architects have had to be consulted about additions and enlargements to the complex, and the resulting mélange reminds one of the campuses.

John M. Johansen, of New York, designed the Mummers' Theatre, opened in 1970, another contribution of urban renewal to downtown Oklahoma City. The local firm of Seminoff, Bowman and Bode supervised construction. Built of cast concrete, its blocks of unit theatres are joined by brightly painted wooden passages, which bridge pools of standing water, equally hospitable to tadpoles and empty paper cups. The building has been called everything from "interesting" to a "boiler house." George Seminoff, senior member of the firm, defines it as "experimentation in planes" and it certainly is.

Seminoff, Bowman and Bode also constructed Fort Everett, the first completely new building of the Medical School complex south of the state capitol. It houses the Dermatology Department of the University of Oklahoma School of Medicine, and the slang name derives from that of the department head, Dr. Mark Allen Everett.

In this structure, as in the Mummers' Theatre, wooden forms were bolted together and liquid concrete poured between them to form walls—another innovation in building. When the forms were removed the imprints of planks and bolts remained in the concrete, forming a textured surface.

Fort Everett, it may be said, is aging well, and the concrete is taking on a deeper tone within the past two years.

Seminoff, Bowman and Bode designed and built the entire campus complex of Oral Roberts University at Tulsa. This is considered by other architects to be one of the finest examples of modern architecture in the United States.

Much of the construction of the Oklahoma State University at Stillwater is red brick and white stone classic revival in style, but the edifice complex refuses to be downed, and several high-rise dormitory towers soar starkly above the warm, ivy-covered graciousness of the Student Center.

And yet, this experimentation and eclecticism are completely Oklahoman. There was once an Indian powwow at which the master of ceremonies announced over the loud speaker:

"You'll have to forgive us if we goof sometimes, folks. When we do something traditional for the first time, it doesn't always go just the way we expect it to."

And that is Oklahoma. We are still doing traditional things for the first times, and sometimes we goof, but we go on. We stake our architectural claims, and, by God, we hold them. If anyone wants conformity and consistency, let him go elsewhere.

CHAPTER 11

FASHIONS AND CHANGES

We do not want to give the impression that only the oil barons and their museums were responsible for bring Culture —with a capital "C," in the sense of bringing the plumbing indoors and of looking at the right kind of paintings—to Oklahoma. On the contrary, many settlers modeled their behavior particularly on that of other newcomers to the state.

There was the Baltimore Belle, for instance. In 1904, she married a young gentleman of good taste and standing and came with him to the new territory where he would make his fortune. Her trousseau and her tableware were elaborate and expensive, and her linen chest included, among other things, one dozen of the finest Brussels lace doilies.

Before 1900, Oklahoma had been almost solidly fundamentalist Protestant. A few Anglican and Roman Catholic missions had struggled among various Indian groups, to little effect. But the Baltimore Belle and her husband were Anglicans born and bred, and, with a small nucleus of the likeminded, they assembled an Episcopal group in Oklahoma

City. The mission grew to a parish in little over a year, and sponsored other missions in different parts of the city. In time, a missionary bishop was appointed to minister to diocesan affairs, and the first stone church, still standing, much enlarged, in good repair and constant use, became St. Paul's Pro-Cathedral, and later Cathedral proper.

Naturally, the creation of a mission diocese called for some social observance, and the Baltimore Belle sent out invitations to her closest friends to attend a dinner at her home, with the bishop and his wife. The Baltimore Belle, for the first time, had the pleasure of unpacking her linen chest and of setting a properly formal dinner for her guests.

In due course, the dessert was served—ice cream molds in the form of Easter lilies, on the Brussels lace doilies. And while the hostess watched, stunned, the bishop, engrossed in conversation with the lovely lady on whose right he sat, calmly, obliviously, ate the lace doily, which had been starched to a crisp, and could well be confused with the dessert proper. Once his hostess started to interfere; then she held her peace. She went through the rest of the dinner grieving for the loss of her "set" of doilies, praying the bishop would not develop indigestion, and, while outwardly poised, in an inner state of complete confusion and turmoil. Thus mere good manners and tact had a part in Oklahoma.

It was a time for formal entertaining everywhere, and Oklahoma was no exception. Ladies, who could, imported their clothes from New York or Chicago. For those who could not afford such luxuries, there was an abundance of dressmakers and milliners in Tulsa, Muskogee, Oklahoma City, Shawnee and Sulphur, among other cities, comparable to the "little milliners and dressmakers" of eastern cities.

In the central northwestern part of Oklahoma City and the

lovely, rolling, wooded hilly area southeast of central Tulsa, mansions were built. They were of all styles; the development uniformity had not yet manifested itself to architects except to those who turned out "row houses" in eastern cities, for people of limited incomes. Oklahoma mansions were highly individual. Architects were brought from Europe, employed from firms in eastern cities, and the upper-income homes boasted thirty to forty rooms, grand ballrooms included, without counting the three or four bathrooms per dwelling. This in cities where the poverty sections today still unashamedly flaunt their outdoor toilets.

Victorian Gothic, Greek Classic, Georgian Revival, even Tudor half-timbered dwellings occupied city lots fifty by one hundred feet, and occupied every inch of most of them. Here and there a property owner, like Henry Overholser of Oklahoma City, bought a quarter of a city block and surrounded his yellow Victorian-Gothic home with gardens. William Hales went even further; his Mediterranean country mansion was built on a quarter section northeast of the city proper. Overholser controlled the city's entertainment business: opera house, vaudeville house and, later, motion picture theatres.

And then, later, there was the Hales mansion in town. Mr. Hales had made his fortune trading horses and mules to the United States Army during World War I. His classic revival home, of white marble, rose on a quarter of a city block one block south of the Overholser dwelling. It had forty rooms, all carpeted with fabrics imported from Europe, and a central hall which housed, along with knights in armor, Göbelein tapestries and Florentine bronzes, a magnificent organ. True, no one knew how to play the organ, but there it was, its pipes rising to the railing of the second-story balcony that surrounded the hall and providing wonderful slides for the Hales children and their friends. Looking back, one hopes the carpets would have been thick enough to cushion a possible fall. The Hales house has since become the archiepiscopal palace of the Roman Catholic diocese of Oklahoma.

The Hales country house has become a church-endowed college. The Overholser house is to be purchased by the Oklahoma Chapter of the American Institute of Architecture for preservation as the most perfect example of its kind in the Middle West. The red-brick home of former District Judge Roy Heffner was presented to the Oklahoma Heritage Corporation in 1970 and converted into a museum. The old Edwards home, once the scene of dances and practically a teenager's heaven, has been replaced by a shopping center, but the land is still the property of the Edwards family. Carriage houses became garages; the owners moved into smaller quarters as they grew older. *Sic transit gloria mundi.*

But the years just after World War I, until the Depression of the thirties set in, were booming. Henry Overholser opened the Delmar Gardens, a real German beer garden except for the movies it showed, in the open space of Sheridan (then Grand) Avenue, Oklahoma City, between his Overholser Theatre and Charles Colcord's magnificent office building, still one of the finest examples of *art nouveau* architecture in the United States, and still standing, all twelve stories of it, in good condition and good use, despite surrounding urban renewal.

Directly across the street, east of the Colcord Building, was another architectural gem that is now gone. This was the Baum Building, an exact reproduction (in Oklahoma marble, of course!) of the Palace of the Doges in Venice.

Once upon a time one could stand on the tenth-floor fire escape of the Colcord Building, and peer a scary distance down into the Delmar Gardens, to sneak a view of the movie being shown.

Other things were visible from that tenth-floor fire escape. One block north was Rothschild's where the rich Osages shopped. One could see chauffeur-driven Marions, Pierce-Arrows, and Reos arrive at the door of the store, and from them dismounted Osage women, swathed in multicolored blankets from Pendleton, Oregon, to do their shopping. One impressive thing about these women was their shoes. Blanketed or shawled, according to the weather, they were always shod in the finest, highest-heeled, pointed-toed opera pumps to be had anywhere.

For now there were oil-rich Indians in Oklahoma. Oil had been found under the bluestem grass of the Osage Reservation just before World War I. The Osages, shrewd Siouans that they were, divided the subsoil wealth into "headrights," one going to each man, woman and child on the tribal rolls. Every quarter year each Osage received his share—and spent it anyway he liked. Osage cars were longer and shinier than any others; Osage women more finely dressed; Osage men, in their inevitable blue serge business suits, handmade boots "by Justin of San Antonio," high-crowned indented black Stetson hats, and the Pendleton blankets they wore instead of overcoats, were more elegantly clothed than any other Oklahoman men.

Prostitutes, bootleggers and dope peddlers set up shop in Pawhuska hotels on payment days, and often obligingly cashed headright checks for their patrons. Tragedies followed; white men and women married Osages, took out life insurance policies on their spouses, and then cold-bloodedly did away with them. It took the clerks of the Bureau of Indian

Affairs office in Pawhuska many years to break and reveal the scandals.

At the same time, a guardian system was instituted, and each Osage placed under the watchful care of a non-Indian keeper. In the cases of bankers and insurance men, particularly, this system was convenient. Honest guardians—there were some—saw that Osage children were sent out of Oklahoma for education, safely removed from Oklahoma's perils. Also, of course, from their own familes.

Some of the Osage students, like the ballerina sisters Maria and Marjorie Tallchief, never returned to live. They were happier and more closely identified with life elsewhere. Others came back as lawyers, oil geologists or, in the case of John Joseph Mathews, a Rhodes scholar who went from Pawhuska, Oklahoma, to Oxford, as writers. Mr. Mathews' stepson, also a writer, lives in Paris, France, and writes about Pawhuska.

The early 1900s were a time when Oklahoma earned a reputation as a good collective theatrical audience. True, Oklahoma City was a "sit on their hands town," as the audience hardly applauded, but Tulsa, Pawhuska, Lawton, and most particularly Muskogee and McAlester attracted the finest talent and responded joyously. Even Louis Graveure, Schumann-Heink, Pavlova, Paderewski and the child actress Helen Hayes did not scorn Oklahoma City, however. Its audiences might sit on their hands, but they sat on them in the Overholser Opera House.

One remembers the thrill of being taken by one's ballet teacher backstage to meet Madame Pavlova and to be presented with a rose by her. Such was Madame's custom with any little girl presented to her, but this recipient did not find that out till many years later, and the thrill remains.

In the mid-twenties, both Oklahoma City and Tulsa had resident stock companies, and a young man named Lee Tracy played juvenile leads in Oklahoma City's Criterion Theatre —the one that was distinguished by its starlight effect of small electric bulbs in the ceiling that dimmed to blackness as the curtain rose. Yes, one could have much that was good in the way of formal entertainment in Oklahoma in the years between the wars.

Less formally, there was the Ringling Brothers-Barnum & Bailey Circus which paraded down many of Oklahoma's main streets with its gilt and glitter and stomach-clutching, thundering calliope, and the Sells-Floto Circus which wintered in Hugo, Oklahoma, and attracted many natives to its ranks. Hugo is still "the circus city." There were county fairs and at least three state fairs: in Muskogee, Tulsa and Oklahoma City, each with its "midway" and "rides." The midways were forbidden territory for well-brought-up little girls, but they must have been thrilling, judging from the fleeting glimpses caught as one hurried past them on the way to the stock pavilion. For then as now the chief focus of interest was livestock—horses, cattle and the mules their breeders boasted were as fine as any in Missouri or Australia. The smell of stock dung mingles in memory's nostrils with mustard, dust and cheap perfume—a nostalgia-producing odor to be found nowhere else.

Rodeo was beginning. It was thoroughly disorganized at first, not the highly commercial exhibition it is now. It had come out of the trick riding of the Miller Brothers' One Hundred and One Ranch Show, the Mulhall family show, which was an off-shoot of Millers', the Pawnee Bill and Two Bills (Buffalo and Pawnee) Shows. All originated in Oklahoma and traveled the world around.

Probably the most spectacular of the Wild West shows was the Millers'. It took its name from the ranch the Millers owned, south of Ponca City, and it featured buffalo, mustangs, elephants, camels, beautiful young lady riders and Indians. All kinds of Indians, but mainly Poncas. There was young Bill Rogers, as he was then called, just starting out with his trick roping act. There was the "greatest cowman of them all," the Negro Bill Pickens.

It was Pickens who invented bull-dogging steers. He would leap from his horse to the steer's back, clutch an ear with his hand and seize the animal's nose in his mouth and wrestle the beast to the ground. When the Society for the Prevention of Cruelty to Animals descended on him for brutally biting the steers, Pickens smiled broadly. He had no teeth. The SPCA retired, defeated. He has just been admitted, posthumously, to the National Cowboy Hall of Fame in Oklahoma City, the first Negro so distinguished.

Everyone who was anyone, from King Edward VII of England and President Theodore Roosevelt down, visited the Miller ranch when they visited the United States or Oklahoma. In addition to the livestock, there were rich experimental orchards which flourished in the limestone soil, pastures knee-deep in the alfalfa which Bill Murray had introduced to the state, irrigation ditches and flowing streams, and a living picture of the West that never was, no matter how badly the white man wanted it to be. Even the Indians were tame.

There was The Great White House, not a ranch house in the usual sense, but a white-stuccoed pseudo-Mediterranean fifty-room dwelling, whose long dining room could, and often did, seat a hundred persons at a serving. A porticoed, deep porch ran around the four sides of the building to guarantee coolness in the days before air conditioning. Artesian wells

6. An Oklahoma homestead, circa 1894.
Courtesy of Oklahoma Historical Society.

7. The Robertson sisters: standing, Mrs. Augusta Moore; seated, left to right, Miss Alice M. Robertson, Mrs. Grace Merriman.
Courtesy of Oklahoma Historical Society.

8. Alice M. Robertson in the House of Representatives, with Speaker of the House Joseph Cannon.
Courtesy of Oklahoma Historical Society.

9. Mrs. Ann Eliza Worcester Robertson. Courtesy of Oklahoma Historical Society.

10. Oklahoma City, April 22, 1910. Courtesy of Oklahoma Historical Society.

11. Old North, the oldest building used for higher education, Central State University, Edmond, Oklahoma.
Courtesy of Central State University.

furnished a plentiful supply of water. Beneath the porch, which was raised a story above the ground, and approached by a majestic flight of white limestone stairs, was the Trading Post. It carried not only the usual hardware, dry goods and groceries, but also stocked Indian crafts and handmade lariats and miniature saddles for the benefit of visitors who might like "something to take home to the children."

Again the glories of the world have passed. The Miller empire crumbled under the onslaughts of the thirties; first, financial depression which left audiences unable to pay for lavish entertainment, and then the dust bowl, which dried up the wells, winds that blasted down the trees and burned out the alfalfa, and finally fire, which destroyed the upper part of the ranch house. In 1939, Zack, the last surviving Miller brother and the greatest showman of them all, was left partially paralyzed, sheltered by the porch roof, hopefully waiting for some kind soul to drive by and buy a souvenir. Then even the highway was moved, so it no longer ran in front of the house, and, like his world, Zack collapsed and died.

But in its day The Great White House stood proudly on its hill, welcoming breezes and visitors, a landmark visible for miles.

To detail all the Wild West shows would be to write another book. Let the memories of the Millers, Bill Pickens and his gleaming pink maw, and Will Rogers' twirling rope suffice for all of them. It was only at The Great White House that Edward VII, King of England, and Theodore Roosevelt, President of the United States, could stand side by side on the cool porch, waiting for the summons to the dining room.

Nowadays rodeo is a competitive sport, and the National American Rodeo Cowboys Association holds its week-long series of battles in Oklahoma City, with suitable high jinks accompanying the celebration at the Cowboy Hall of Fame and Western Heritage Center, on Persimmon Hill, towering over Highway 66. Jim Shoulders, of Henryetta, Oklahoma, is renowned as the greatest competitive rodeo rider of the world, but others are not far behind him. It's show business again.

CHAPTER 12

THE BURIED CITY

The Chinese and the railroads crisscrossed America together. The Chinese would do such menial work as cooking, dishwashing and cleaning. They would lay ties. They were hardy, polite, industrious, and they could seldom talk back because few of them spoke English. The great ambition of most Chinese seemed to be to earn and save enough money to import their relatives to the United States, in defiance of immigration laws.

Many and varied—from the outright obscene to the plain silly—are the western stories concerning Chinese. The truth was that the Chinese kept to themselves; their culture was rich and old, and they had no need for contacts with other men. They were sufficient alone.

In the 1920s, when Oklahoma City was still comparatively a small town, with only one high school, every student in that school knew, beyond the question of a doubt, that there was a Chinese city underlying the business district, a few blocks to the south. The high schoolers knew that tunnels underground followed the streets above, and that a whole community of Chinese lived there in secret.

How they knew, who told whom what are as secret as the city itself. They just knew. There were no Chinese students in high school to furnish authoritative information and addresses. But every high schooler knew where the blue door opened out of an alley onto a staircase leading underground to the buried city. There was a cemetery and there was an opium den and there was a Buddhist temple, and their existence was as sure as that of the state capitol or the high school themselves.

In time, Chinese appeared above ground, buying houses in ordinary residential districts, opening restaurants which served not only delicious but immaculately clean food, enrolling their own children in the three high schools that now existed, sending students to the university and the medical school and, finally, emerging in their own right as citizens. Only the old men and women wore the long gowns and flat-soled slippers of tradition. Younger men and women dressed like everyone else. The underground city (now that there was no single high school to serve as an information center) was not only buried, but forgotten.

Came the dawn of urban renewal in 1969. The city fathers decided that the business district had not only been abandoned in favor of shopping centers, but had become disgracefully run down. Why not clean out the whole place, tear down the Huckins Hotel along with many other buildings, and construct a gigantic convention center? A new hotel could be built for visitors.

And so the work of demolition began. The wreckers' balls were aided by a little well-located arson, and Main Street certainly no longer looked the way it used to. And there, in the alley paralleling Main and Sheridan (as Grand Avenue had become), was a blue-painted door, dulled and faded and dimmed by time and weather, but still there in the back of one of the old three-story false-front business buildings. And still padlocked, with a Chinese lock so curious that it has become a museum piece. The lock and the straps that held it had to be torn from the door.

Leading down, before the amazed eyes of the wrecking crew, was a flight of stairs—stone stairs, well-constructed and of convenient width and depth, laid evidently by a mason who knew what he was doing and had done his best.

Work stopped on the spot, and the former Mayor of Oklahoma City George Shirk was sent for to examine the find. Mr. Shirk was president of the Oklahoma Historical Society. With a party that included reporters, photographers and his sister Lucyl, Mayor Shirk marched forward, monumentally, down the steps.

There it all was, as it had been since the buried city was abandoned. An opium den, with pipes and cakes of opium on the table. Living quarters for families and for single men. The Buddhist temple, its walls papered with faded gilt instead of the Chinese newspapers that covered the other rooms. Even the cemetery remained, its graves flattened by time, its bodies melted into the earth. Tunnels underground led to the sites of the first Chinese restaurants.

And like all high school graduates of his generation, Mayor Shirk, a distinguished historian in his own right, mused, "We should have believed ourselves all the time."

CHAPTER 13

SELECTIVE COSMOPOLITANISM

In 1873, coal was discovered in the Choctaw Nation, not far from McAlester's Trading Post, just north of the site of present McAlester. McAlester was a Scots trader who had married into a prominent Choctaw family, and he could see the advantages of the coal beds, for he was familiar with bituminous coal from Glasgow.

McAlester did not import Scots miners when he discovered that the Choctaws, and later the Chickasaws, were not interested in mining. Instead, he brought over an entire Italian village because the people had previous mining experience which he admired, and settled the families in what was, naturally enough, to become Pittsburgh County. The Indians farmed, the Italians mined, McAlester traded and everyone was happy.

No one foresaw then the battles that would arise between the Choctaw tribe and the Choctaw Mining Company, or that similar confusion would occur later over the Chickasaw mineral rights. As had happened to the Cherokees, old feuds were revived and perpetuated once more. The question of tribal vs. corporate vs. individual rights has not yet been settled. The recently instituted custom of tribal elections instead of presidential appointments of chiefs has only made the struggle more bitter.

But the Italians were not greatly concerned by the multilingual tribal battles raging over their heads. They built their homes, drew their weekly pay checks and were allowed to send their children to the schools of the Choctaw Nation, where everybody was taught in English.

Eventually the generation of Italian miners learned enough to realize that they had one great and enviable asset of their own—food. Italian groceries and food-importing houses were unknown in Indian Territory, but the Italian ladies made do with what they had and sent home for what they could not find. The hillsides of the Choctaw country had already proved hospitable to native wild grapes, and they were equally accommodating when root stocks were sent from overseas and Italian grapes were planted or, later, grafted on the native vines. In bone-dry, prohibition-bound Indian Territory a healthy wine-making industry grew, flourished and gained fame.

When the Italian families were questioned about their possibly illegal activities, they were blandly responsive. Wine was not whiskey, they explained. It was food—even the children drank it with their meals instead of water, and it was certainly better for the little ones than tea or coffee. Milk as a beverage had no more place in Choctaw and Chickasaw diets than it had in Italian ones, so no one even thought of suggesting cows' milk for drinking. Goats' milk, yes, that the Italians had in abundance. How else would one make cheese or have roast kid for Sunday dinner? Goats' milk was an absolute necessity for certain kinds of cooking, and besides, the goats grazed on the undergrowth on the hillsides and cleared more land that could then be planted to vines. Goats were a tangible asset. They were also, as the flocks grew and flourished, sometimes a considerable nuisance.

It is a little surprising to an eastern visitor to be told that the first western outpost of Italian cooking existed in towns with such names as McAlester, Krebs and Hartshorne—the last two named for prominent Choctaw chiefs.

These are not the "pizzarias" that sprang up from Lawton to Tahlequah and back by way of Muskogee, Tulsa, Oklahoma City and El Reno, as far west as Clinton, Cordell and Elk City. These restaurants are good solid northern Italian farmsteads, built solidly of native stone, where food is cooked and served in the kitchen when the dining room and living room become too crowded. Reservations are necessary days in advance.

The food, too, is that of the northern Italian hill country, and is seasoned with discretion. Pastas are still homemade. State law forbids butchering any animal under six months of age, but if a calf or a *cabrillo*, barely able to stagger along the hillsides, meets with an accident, can its owner be blamed? True veal scallopine or marsala, and true roast *cabrillo* are still to be had in the old Choctaw Nation.

It would not be fair to mention food in the Choctaw Nation without a passing glance at the Charles Wesley Hotel, in Broken Bow. Broken Bow, also in hill country, was settled after the Civil War by Southerners escaping the wrecked South. Here the food was in the best southern tradition: fried chicken that crunched with every bite; cat fish and corn dodgers or hush puppies; every known variety of wild and garden greens in season; biscuits so light they had to be caught in midair before they floated off the serving tray. Everything was served "family style," with the guests seated in facing rows at long tables, and platters and trays passing up and down the table and out to the kitchen to be refilled as requested. To one who thinks chain restaurants serve "southern" food, the Charles Wesley was a revelation and a haven for travelers. But today the "southern" food of the Charles Wesley has been replaced by standard motel cooking.

Prague, established as a community in 1902, and Yukon, settled during the Alaskan gold rush of 1891, straddle Oklahoma City. Both are Czech settlements, founded and still in large measure occupied by immigrants and their descendants.

Both Prague and Yukon maintain native tradition in their dress for special occasions, folk songs, dances and Kolache festivals.

One of the special specials of the Oklahoma Festival of the Arts, held in Oklahoma City each spring, is the Czech booth. The women bake delicacies for months in advance, holding them in freezers until the time comes to sell them. There are native crafts on display and for sale, and orders will be taken for special native costumes. Meanwhile, folk dancers twirl and whirl on an outdoor stage, to the music of violins and accordions. Citizens of both towns participate.

Prague is the national shrine of the Holy Infant of Prague, and the festival honoring the Holy Infant is held there in the spring. In Yukon, almost solidly Protestant, the festival is held in the fall, sometime between Halloween and Thanksgiving.

There are other more isolated ethnic pockets in Oklahoma. Between Colony and Corn and stretching as far north as Geary are the German Mennonites, settled in the region since

1896. They are famous farmers, who can make every inch of infertile soil produce. Not strict-rule Mennonites, they mingle and marry with members of other groups. Each year at round-up time the German Mennonite men butcher out a tenth of each herd, and the meat is cooked into soup by the women and canned for distribution to the needy. It is a notable charity, and one that unobtrusively reaches many parts of the world.

The true "hook and eye" Amish farm the country north of Weatherford, and keep strictly to themselves except when they drive to town in their black buggies on Saturdays, to transact business. Because they cling to their old dress and language, as well as to their religious convictions, these "Germans" are somewhat feared and avoided by other western Oklahomans. It is possible to drive from Cheyenne to Weatherford and identify the Amish farms scattered among the allotments of the Arapahos. The Amish have barns and fences, and the Indians too often use their front yards as graveyards for dead automobiles.

We cannot leave the subject of ethnic communities without reference to the "Freedmen's towns." These communities were established by the freed slaves of the Five Civilized Tribes and other freed Negroes, and are maintained by their descendants.

All Freedmen, Negroes belonging to Indian members of the Five Civilized Tribes, were enrolled separately and often given many of the privileges of their former Indian owners, at the end of the Civil War. A few of their descendants have intermarried with Indians, but the towns remain almost solidly black, and are practically closed to whites. We have students in our university classes who came originally from the towns of Boley, Taft and Mounds, and a few have been willing to carry on research on the subject of Negro Freedmen with us, but the towns are still closed to us. Sometimes people who are actually three-quarters Indian by blood prefer to identify with the Negro population. Prospective guides, who offer to accompany and introduce us, always seem to be busy doing something else when the time comes to leave. It is a tantalizing research subject, and the first one that has ever baffled either one of us, let alone both.

In conclusion we can say that while Oklahoma is less cosmopolitan than any eastern state, it has a selective cosmopolitanism of its own. There was the tight little United Kingdom of men who designed and constructed the state capitol building.

There was the father who, born in England and with an English name, had practiced law in the Italian quarter of Chicago and learned the language so well that his clients altered his name to "Ricardo Marriotti" and taught him to cook.

His daughter still remembers the big Ventura farmhouse west of Oklahoma City where the grapevines grew, and one sat on the front porch with "Grandmama" Ventura and sipped the good red wine and ate bananas. The skins of the fruit went to the goats: Teresina, Rosina and "Carrruso." And while one sat one learned of the herbs in the garden and their use in the kitchen, to make drawn work, and above all, to laugh and sing.

Then the men arose from the wine cellars, bottles for the coming year selected and legal questions settled, and there was the slow drive to the Marriott home in the dusk, with Joe Ventura at the wheel and with "Grandpapa" Ventura leaning over the back of the front seat and singing most of Verdi on the way. It was a short course in Italian culture for someone growing up among the farmers and tradesmen of central Oklahoma.

And there was "Gran'ma" Sarczyski, mother-in-law of Max Cunningham's engineering partner, born in the old-country City of Prague and struggling to learn a little English, even from children. And Janet and Ruth Sawicki, of the second generation, social case worker and legal secretary, whose mother conscientiously taught them the crafts she had learned before she left Poland as a bride. The melting pot is bubbling more than a little around the edges.

CHAPTER 14

THE BAD OLD DAYS

We have hinted, in other places, that integration did not prove a simple, easy process in Oklahoma. Looking back, in terms of personalities, it seems to have been even rougher than it appeared at the time.

In 1921, the Tulsa race riot took place and rocked not only that city and the state, but the nation. Rural Negroes had moved into the cities by thousands between 1916 and 1920, attracted by the chances of better paying jobs than the cotton fields offered, and by the hope of better education for their children. Both hopes were only partially, if at all, fulfilled.

We are back again to Max Cunningham. A bond issue had been floated to raise money to bridge the Arkansas River and join Tulsa and Red Fork, which by then was known as West Tulsa. The contract had been let, and the contractor employed Max's younger brother, Phillip, as supervising engineer.

The Cunninghams had come from an Ohio town where there was no segregation of whites and Negroes. Their grandfather had run a station on the underground railway, hiding escaped slaves under the floor of his general merchandise store. The brothers had gone to school with Negroes and played football with Negro teammates and opponents.

The Cunninghams disagreed about many things, but on some they took a firm united stand. They were more gifted in profanity than any other men their niece has ever known, they were firmly convinced that enough roads and bridges would solve all the world's problems, and that if a man could do an adequate day's work the color of his skin was immaterial.

Phillip was living in Tulsa with his wife and their three children, aged four, three and two. Because the children were a handful for their mother, Max, who made decisions for all the family, sent for his older niece to stay with her aunt and help with the children. There was a maid, but she was kept too busy to have much time to spare for dusting, storytelling and other odd jobs. A good husky eleven-year-old, who had already learned to cook, was a distinct advantage to the household.

Nobody knows how the riot started. The usual, and most widely believed story is that a Negro man joggled against a white woman in a downtown elevator, which he was operating. The old, tired cry of "Rape!" went up, and an already tense situation exploded.

Fires, rock throwing and looting (whites were not innocent of this) began that night in downtown Tulsa. By morning, the recently elected governor, Jack Walton, had called out the state National Guard. Before the Guardsmen could reach the Tulsa Armory from different parts of the city and outlying communities, the whites had invaded the Negro section of the city, and full-scale war had broken out. Phillip Cunningham removed his family from the city to the construction camp—a delightful outing for the children—and placed his

Negro foreman, the man in charge of dynamiting rocks out of the riverbanks, in charge of them, too.

For three days and two nights the family waited, wondering if there would be a home to return to. The nights were lighter than the days, for smoke obscured the summer sun, but flames lighted the night sky. Then came word that five thousand Negroes were marching on Tulsa from Muskogee, to complete the work of demolition.

Women and children were stowed in the dynamite storage cave, from which the dynamite had been removed. By this time some of the workmen had managed to slip into town and bring their families out, so about twenty people waited underground for the invasion.

The Cunningham men mounted their horses—every man had a horse of some sort in those days, even if he also had an automobile—and rode out to survey the situation. A man afoot is no man at all, and a man in a car can be mighty lonely and in considerable danger, but a man on horseback is a *man*—a *caballero*—and can command respect and sometimes obedience. They rode eastward, down the road toward Muskogee, to see what was happening.

In later years, retelling the story, they found another common bond. The telling always ended with the words "There wasn't a soul around. There never had been. It was all a false alarm." "Still," their niece adds, "these alarms of fire can be upsetting."

To turn to Governor Walton, whose National Guard had finally contained the rioting so that people could take up their lives again, he was and remains a controversial figure in Oklahoma's history. A real estate man and engineer, he figured prominently in the state's political circles from the beginning.

After the Tulsa riot the Ku Klux Klan was revived and

rode again, to take vengeance on the Negroes for the thirty-three persons killed in the street fighting (most of them were Negroes, and probably shouldn't have been counted by the standards of the day), but it gave certain population elements a gorgeous excuse to erect flaming crosses—sometimes flaming crucifixes to which living men were lashed—on hilltops; to frighten tenant farmers, and generally bully the state.

They also paraded at night through city streets, robed and hooded in white, with the initials KKK in red across their backs. One child of those days remembers watching such a procession file by in absolute, shuffling silence. She clutched her parents' hands, shivering, until a sign held high by one of the marchers caught her eye. "We Are Men from Every Walk Of Life" it proclaimed. Then she began to watch the marchers' feet. Cowboy boots, business shoes, high-laced construction boots, even Indian moccasins moved over the pavement.

The state legislature met in special session. It impeached Governor Walton on several counts, among them one that he had put down the Tulsa riot "by use of armed force," and another that he had not put down the Ku Klux Klan. Then someone discovered that the Governor himself was not only a member of the Klan, but was high in its councils. The impeachment became a conviction, and Lieutenant Governor Martin Trapp, a mild but determined lawyer, inherited the mess. He raised funds to rebuild the wrecked portions of Tulsa, and he also, "by use of armed force," did away with the Klan. Peace descended long enough for the reactionism of the twenties and the Depression of the thirties to set in, but Governor Trapp left a solvent state (for the first time) when he went out of office.

CHAPTER 15

NAUGHTY, NAUGHTY

At the end of World War I, in 1919, a financial and social upheaval, such as often follows a war, set in all over the country. Men were back from the war. They were no longer singing "Over There" and "It's a Long Long Way to Tipperary," but they had almost reached the point of "Brother, Can You Spare a Dime?"

Veterans banded together and marched on Washington to demand service bonuses. Even Oklahoma's war hero, the most-decorated soldier of the war, a Choctaw, Joseph Oklahombi, joined the ranks that camped on the Mall, only to be dispersed by a young and efficient colonel named Douglas MacArthur. The veterans trudged home bonusless, industries retooled and absorbed them, and a boom was on.

This was not a time of true desperation. That was to come later. President Warren G. Harding set an example of relaxed living by playing poker with his cronies in the White House, sipping legally forbidden highballs—for national Prohibition of alcohol had been part of the puritan reaction to the war's ending—and generally disported himself until his death in San Francisco from food poisoning, in mid-term.

After Harding's death Vice-President Calvin Coolidge, a Vermont Yankee, took over the Administration, and things generally quieted down a bit. Oh, there had been high-level scandals during Harding's administration, such as the Teapot Dome oil appropriation on the Crow Indian Reservation, but that was in Montana and a long way from Oklahoma. Oklahomans relaxed and enjoyed themselves.

Moonshine distilling and bootlegging were well-established Oklahoma institutions. The hills and woods of eastern Oklahoma had been the happy hunting grounds of revenue men for nearly a century, and after Prohibition was written into the United States Constitution, the custom spread to the less sheltered and concealing parts of the state.

A bootlegger was a man who stuffed his cowboy boots— purposely made loose-fitting—with pint and half-pint flat bottles. A moonshiner distilled a mash of corn and perhaps a little wheat to extract the famous white lightning. There were some moonshiners who were so proud of their products that they had the glass jars from which they sold made to order, bearing their names. It need hardly be said that these are collectors' items today.

Along the East and West coasts, and the Canadian and Mexican borders, smuggling of "the real good stuff" was constant. Sometimes the real good stuff consisted of white lightning delicately tinted with tea, but it brought ten times the price of the homemade product. It was also a prestige item—a status symbol.

The poor might have their homemade "Choc" or "Choctaw" beer, which was lethal if it blew up and hit the ceiling, and people of European ancestry who were not too far removed from the old country produced wine from Oklahoma's wild grapes, thus further thinning out the underbrush in the Cross Timbers. But a man of position should have, and tried to have, some of the real stuff around in case important guests should drop in.

Such a man was Max Cunningham. In the mid-twenties he attended an engineering conference in Chicago, with a side trip to Detroit where "scotch" crossed the border from Windsor, Ontario, and he brought back a suitcase full. Absent-mindedly, he packed his checkbook—name and address on each check, in those days another status symbol and not a computing necessity—in the lid of the same suitcase. He did not remember the checkbook until the porter dropped the suitcase, with a resounding thud, on the station platform in Oklahoma City. Mr. Cunningham, shocked into memory of that checkbook, simply walked away from suitcase, alcoholic reek, and all, and next time traveled north on the Rock Island, in case the Santa Fe passenger agent should have too long a memory.

Bathtub gin never made much headway in Oklahoma. By most southern and English standards, gin was a stable boy's drink and not for gentlemen. Besides, who knew? Someone in the family might decide to take a bath and that would be hard on the gin even if it were rescued from going down the drain. No, wines extracted from all local varieties of fruits took the place of the real stuff in Oklahoma entertaining, where whiskey was preferred to all substitutes, if it were to be had.

The middle 1920s were not as coy about their wildness as the 1890s, but what they lacked in demureness they made up for in vitality. Women's hair was cut short—one of us had the first "Eton cut" in Oklahoma City when she was in high school—skirts were shorter, although they never reached the height of the mini-skirts in the 1960s and 1970s. Camisoles and corsets disappeared, to be replaced by one-piece garments called "teddy bears," which performed the joint functions of underdrawers and slips. Women took to wearing pajamas. Without supporters on the teddy bears women rolled their stockings to or below their knees, and wore shoes with high spiked heels.

Feminine beauty had never undergone so much improvement since the days of Marie Antoinette. Respectable women had confined their cosmetics for a century to a cake of soap and a dusting of cornstarch or talcum powder. Now a blob of rouge on either cheekbone, a painted, pouting bee-stung pair of lips produced with lipstick, and even a smudge of color around the eyes became acceptable. There were day creams, night creams and hand lotions. Face powder became fashionable in a variety of colors.

The permanent-wave machine had been invented to make straight hair curly. It was a fearsome object, massive in structure, and equipped with dangling spools attached to wires. The hair was wound tightly around the spools, the mass was soaked with chemicals which *smelled* as if they would produce results, and the electric current was turned on. Timing was vastly important—too much heat was likely to remove the hair in hanks, too little to leave it unchanged, and the exact amount produced a tightly curled mass, which felt a good deal like hay, but was highly fashionable.

Naturally, a lady could not sit for hours under such a contraption in a barber shop. The barber shop was and remained inviolably a man's world. So female vanity was pampered to by hair dressers and manicurists (some women daringly had their nails colored to match their lipsticks), and a rash of "beauty salons" gave employment to untrained, semi-trained and capable "beauty operators." Not until the end of the decade did Oklahoma establish licensing laws for "beauticians."

And women *smoked*. It had been customary in Europe and some parts of the eastern United States for women to smoke cigarettes (sometimes violet-scented) or cigarillos in private, but now the brazen hussies flaunted their vice on the streets, in cars—wherever they happened to be.

Women's legs came out of hiding and men's legs did too; men who played golf began wearing the knickerbockers called plus fours—first on the golf courses and then on the streets and in offices. Not until the craze for men's shorts in the fifties was there such a hullabaloo about questions of good and bad taste for men.

Women could rationalize their smoking, their abbreviated garments and haircuts. They wanted to be free—to be liberated from the confines of clothes and to be the equals of men in every way. Men did not have the same excuse, and the plus fours were not comfortable anyway. They vanished, and the men succumbed again to long pants. In 1920, the Nineteenth Amendment to the Constitution gave women the right to vote and made them the political equals of males. A few took advantage of their change in status. Oklahoma's unamendable constitution was amended again, to conform with the federal regulations.

In 1924, not by constitutional amendment, but by act of Congress, all Indians in the United States were given the right to vote in federal elections. In Oklahoma they could already vote in local ones. The congressional action was a recognition of Indian participation in World War I. But it took fifty years for Indians to realize that, grandfather clauses or no grandfather clauses, they could vote for senators, congressmen, and presidential electors. Of course, the states still controlled their right to vote in local elections. All the same, a part Kaw Indian, Charles Curtis, became Vice-President of the United States under Hoover, and the florid signature of Houston B. Teehee, a Cherokee, appeared as Treasurer of the United States on a long series of bank notes.

True it is that nothing endures but change. A wild, arm-flinging, leg-pitching dance known as the Charleston swept the country. A girl who lived in Lawton for seven years, Lucille Le Sueur, won the state Charleston contest and went to Hollywood, where she became known as Joan Crawford, and was starred in *Flaming Youth*, a picture made from the novel of the day.

Oklahomans were beginning to appear on the national scene in other fields. Jennie Harris Oliver published slender volumes of poetry of which no one writing in English need be ashamed.

Dora Aydelotte wrote two or three excellent novels of pioneer days. And John Joseph Mathews, returned from the Lafayette Escadrille, wrote the first book to be published by Joseph Brandt at the new University of Oklahoma Press, *Wahkontah*, and with it won a Book-of-the-Month Club award.

Anabel Mraz, daughter of a Hungarian immigrant, also received a rose from Pavlova, under the auspices of the same dancing teacher, Miss Felice Haubiel, and went on the road with Pavlova's *corps de ballet*, finally becoming a ballerina in her own right.

Ralph Rose, whose family ran Oklahoma City's first exclusively confectionery store, and mighty good candy they made, went east to study with Heifetz, who was not much older than Rose, and began a notable career of violin playing and of conducting at Carnegie Hall. He returned in the Depression of the 1930s to become the conductor of the state's first symphony orchestra.

On and on we could go. Dr. Joseph Thoburn (Ph.D.) established a state Historical Society, although it was a long time before the museum and its publications moved out of the Aunt-Martha's-attic, self-glorification stage. Dr. Thoburn conducted the first archaeological "digs" in Oklahoma. He was janitor, preparator, curator, director and editor of the society's magazine. The museum was established in the basement of the Capitol Building, much to the annoyance of the ladies of the D.A.R. who had to climb over, under and around Dr. Thoburn's specimens to reach the stairs. The specimens remained in the basement until the Historical Society erected its own building in the 1930s and the ladies of the D.A.R. were given a hall all their own.

Jazz had come upriver from New Orleans and across the prairies from Chicago, and was being discovered as music, not cacophony. Now it was fashionable not only to dance to such tunes as "Yes Sir, That's My Baby" and "There She Goes, on Her Toes," but to analyze them in musical terms, relating Basin Street blues to the laboriously concocted sonatas of Bach. It was a time when everything had to move and move fast.

A young airman, Charles Lindbergh of Michigan, flew non-stop from New York to Paris with three oranges, a ham sandwich and a kitten. When he returned to the United States, the federal government sent him on a barnstorming tour of the country, to promote what he called "aerrrrrrronautics"—a rolling *r* sound strange to southwestern ears. Lindbergh broke the ground for what was fondly hoped to be the first college-level School of Aeronautics in the United States, on the campus of Oklahoma City University, about where the Angie Smith Memorial Methodist Chapel stands now. It was an outburst of hero worship that never, quite literally, got off the ground.

To write of Oklahoma in the 1920s without mentioning those folk heroes Bonnie Parker and Clyde Barrow, Pretty Boy Floyd, and George (Machine Gun) and Kathryn Kelly would be impossible.

Bonnie and Clyde have been so immortalized in song and on the screen so much that little remains to be said of them. The only things to be added to the tale of two no-longer juvenile delinquents is that when they were finally shot down by "the Law" and their bodies were taken to an undertaker to be prepared for burial, the embalmers were horrified to find that Bonnie's body was decorated from neckline to toe with elaborate tattooing, some of it obscene and some of it simply adornment. Never, they said, had they seen anything like that on a woman—and they hoped they never would again.

Pretty Boy Floyd, like Bonnie and Clyde and their cohorts, was a product of eastern Oklahoma, but he was a loner. He had his headquarters in the Cookson Hills, a notorious hangout for bootleggers and moonshiners, and dealt with both. In the intervals, he robbed banks. He, too, was finally shot down by "the Law" in 1928, and so many sightseers came to his funeral that the satin lining was stripped from his coffin by souvenir collectors.

The Kellys were made of sterner stuff. One night, accompanied by a henchman, they invaded the Oklahoma City home of Charles Urschel, an oil man, who, with his wife, was entertaining friends, Mr. and Mrs. W. R. Larrett. Mr. Urschel and Larrett were marched out of the house with machine guns pointed at them, and loaded into a car in the driveway.

Kathryn Kelly remained behind to tie the two women to their chairs and then joined her husband. Urschel's companion was released in southern Oklahoma City, and made his way to a telephone to report the incident to the police. Urschel, who was known to be a wealthy man, was blindfolded and bound, and driven into the night to be held for a million-dollar ransom.

Urschel had not gained wealth by being stupid. As he lay day after day on a cot, his legs secured and his hands untied only for meals, his eyes constantly blindfolded, he still could listen. Regularly, at set intervals, he heard airplanes fly overhead. He would count slowly to sixty, then ask his guard, whoever it might be, what the time was.

After a week, the ransom was raised and paid. Urschel again was driven into the night and released by the roadside. About an hour later, his business partner picked him up and drove him from a side road in the piny woods of Texas, back to Oklahoma City.

After greeting his wife, and while a square meal was being prepared for him, Urschel called the newly created Federal Bureau of Investigation. To them he described the whole episode, including the flight pattern of the planes he had heard. From this description, the lawmen were able to pinpoint the spot where Urschel had been held and to identify George and Kathryn Kelly, and Mrs. Kelly's mother, who had all made the mistake of returning to their headquarters. The trial was held in the Federal Court in Oklahoma City, after much wrangling between lawyers concerning legal jurisdiction, and the defendants were sentenced to the state penitentiary at McAlester, where they served out their terms, to everyone's surprise. The state Pardon and Parole Board enforced the law in their case.

Oklahoma City held no more charm for Mr. and Mrs. Urschel. With Mrs. Urschel's children, by a previous marriage, they moved home and business to San Antonio, Texas. When Mr. and Mrs. Urschel died, their house and its truly magnificent contents were put up at auction, sold to an anonymous bidder, and returned to the Oklahoma City Art Center by an equally anonymous donor. "After all," said Mr. Urschel's lawyer, who had handled the bidding, "there was no point in saving things for the children. They all had houses and things that were just as good, if not better."

So fortunes were made and lost in Oklahoma in the 1920s. It was a time very much like the 1960s and '70s. Great wealth and abject poverty existed side by side all over the state; crimes ranged from the petty to the magnificent; the drug trade flourished and became federal scandal, and young people, with a war behind them and another dismally predicted ahead, threw off restraints in dress, drinking and general behavior. The thing that strikes us as curious, with the perspective of time as a telescope, is that most people failed to take anything very seriously—until 1929 when the stock market crashed and the Depression began.

PART TWO
The Peoples of It

Carol K. Rachlin to Rex Whistler, Jr., aged ten, "Do you like powwows?" Rex Whistler in reply, "I don't like the dancing part, but I like the peoples of it."

CHAPTER 16

"LET US NOW PRAISE FAMOUS MEN"

It seems best to discuss the men whose portraits stand in the state capitol chronologically, for no more surprising assortment of characters could have existed anywhere. One who might well have been included was omitted as too controversial: Alfalfa Bill Murray, who deserves more space than we have heretofore given him.

Sequoyah, the Lame One, was first in point of time. His father was Nathaniel Gist, or Guest—it has been spelled both ways—an English-descended trader who went to the Cherokees from Baltimore in the late 1700s. Sequoyah, whose English name was George Gist, always claimed to have been born in the same year as the republic, 1776.

Sequoyah's mother was Wuh-tee, the daughter of a prominent Cherokee family, who was related to the Ross family on her mother's side. Even though marriage between Cherokees and whites by tribal custom was held to be legal and binding on both parties, Wuh-tee chose to live with her own people and to raise her son among them, while Nathaniel ranged far and wide on his business pursuits.

The boy was named the Lame One in childhood; perhaps as a result of an accident, or perhaps because of development of tuberculosis of the bone in one leg. The records on this point are incomplete, and Sequoyah himself refused to discuss his handicap.

He grew up entirely in the old, traditional Cherokee life, taught by his mother's father and brothers, and deeply immersed in tribal religion. It has been said, on what grounds we do not know, that he learned not only the religion of healing which was the mainstay of Cherokee life, but also that of witchcraft. This unsupported statement is one we find hard to believe, in view of the many accounts that have come down of Sequoyah's kindness and generosity.

Although he refused to learn his father's language, or even acknowledge for many years that he had a white father, Sequoyah did learn metalworking from a traveling tinsmith. He not only mended pots and pans and kettles, he learned silversmithing. One of his granddaughters, Norah Roper, a teacher in the Sequoyah Orphan Training School at Tahlequah, was buried with a bracelet he had made clasped around her wrist. The workmanship was simple and fine, although the design by then was almost obliterated. The bracelet had been put on her arm in childhood, and she never took it off. Sequoyah's grandson, George Guest, is a cabinetmaker in Muskogee.

As a young man, Sequoyah ranged much as his father had done, up and down the Cherokee Nation East, his pack of tools on his back, looking for work. Eventually he married, and he and his wife set up a home in the hills of southeastern

Tennessee. They had children, the youngest being a little girl, Ahyoka (She Brought It).

The War of 1812, as we have said, provided a heaven-sent opportunity for the Cherokees to take revenge on their habitual enemies, the Creeks. Sequoyah joined the United States forces, perhaps influenced to some degree by Sam Houston. During the war, Sequoyah had an opportunity to see what he called "the talking leaves"; the letters white servicemen received from their families. Even though he could not understand what the men said, he watched them read and discuss the letters, and learned that the papers came from their families and homes. Sequoyah was fired with an idea. If leaves could talk to the white men, why could they not talk to the Cherokees?

Somewhere or other, probably on his way home from the Battle of Horseshoe Bend, Sequoyah found a child's spelling book lying on the road. He had seen books before, in the hands of the white men, so he knew what a book was. As he opened this one, he saw that the first pages were covered with symbols, and that the symbols were repeated, in varying combinations, on the later pages. Some he recognized from the talking leaves the soldiers had received. This, then, was the clue. Make symbols for Cherokee sounds, and he would have talking leaves the Cherokees could use.

For two years Sequoyah worked on his syllabary, for what he developed was not an alphabet in our sense of the word, but a kind of shorthand. His sons were grown and married, and only little Ahyoka was at home. She picked up sheets of sycamore bark on which he could scratch with charcoal, and she sat with him by the hour, endlessly mouthing words that he could reduce to sounds.

Meantime, the garden went untended, the animals were uncared for except for what his wife could do and, last straw for the poor woman, the cabin roof began to leak. After days of nagging, she gathered together the laboriously written sheets of bark and flung them into the fire. It had all gone for nothing.

Without a word, Sequoyah picked up his bag of tinker's tools, his rifle, took Ahyoka by the hand, and walked out of what was by tribal custom his wife's house. The first day he succeeded in shooting a deer, and eventually he soft-tanned the skin. It was more durable material to record on than the bark, and could be rolled up and carried on his back as he and Ahyoka wandered through the countryside where he mended pots and pans and kettles wherever he could find work, living precariously from hand to mouth when he could not. At last he came to the home of a young widow, Sally, who lived with her father and son, Teessee. They were lowland people, and fully aware of the encroachments of white settlement. Sally and Sequoyah were married by tribal custom—after all, his first wife had divorced him in the same way—and the new family set out for the West with others of the Old Settlers.

The two children were of the same age, and Ahyoka taught Teessee reading and writing, as she had learned it from her father. Sally learned, too, and so did her father. They found a place to live, first in Arkansas, and later near the present town of Salina, Oklahoma. Here Sequoyah continued his studies, Sally and her father worked in the garden, Teessee cared for the animals and hunting, and Ahyoka kept house. It was a happy well-adjusted family, in which each had his place and share. The log cabin where they lived still stands inside a stone building as a historical site.

Eventually word of the wonders of reading and writing the Cherokee language were taken back to the still-existent Cherokee Nation in Tennessee and Georgia, by Old Settlers who were visiting their families. Principal Chief John Ross sent for Sequoyah to come and demonstrate his miracle to the Tribal Council. Sequoyah returned East at the bidding of his old friend, taking Ahyoka with him, to the Cherokee capitol, New Echota, Georgia.

Ross was himself only one-quarter Cherokee by blood, and his wife was half white. On the day they were to meet with the Council, Quatie Ross dressed Ahyoka in new clothes from the skin out and John Ross provided her with pen and ink and paper. Both things upset Sequoyah. He was sure the child would be more comfortable in her old clothes, and he knew she had never seen such writing materials before.

Ross stood before the council and dictated a letter in Cherokee to Sequoyah, who, using the pen and ink himself instead of allowing Ahyoka to, wrote it down and left the room. While he limped up and down the grass outside the Council House, waiting for the outcome, Ahyoka took her place before the assembly. Clearly and without hesitation she read aloud what her father had written:

"Ahyoka! [She Brought It!]" Ross cried, and so the child received her woman's name. Her baby name has been forgotten. Sequoyah returned to the Council to set about immediately teaching the Council members the syllabary. As they dispersed, the men taught it to everyone they met. Within two months every Cherokee who was capable of learning it was literate in his own language. A national press had previously been established, and now special fonts of Cherokee type were cast in Boston. The nation awarded Sequoyah a medal, and a salt bed worth, in those days, five hundred dollars a year. It was the only purely literary pension ever awarded in the United States.

Sequoyah was convinced that any Indian language could be written in his syllabary, and indeed his eighty-six characters are no more unwieldy than most shorthand systems. He was also convinced that somewhere there would be an original, basic Indian language, and he spent much time and thought trying to find it. After the western removal, John Ross built Park Hill and the two national seminaries south of Tahlequah, where Tsa-lah-ghi, a reconstructed Cherokee village of the period now stands, and a pageant of the Trail of Tears is performed each summer. Sequoyah and Ross play prominent parts in its cast of characters.

After Sally's death, Sequoyah and two of the sons of his first marriage set out in search of the universal Indian language, traveling west and south. Five-toned Kiowa, which sounds more like Mandarin Chinese than anything else, defeated them. Wichita, Comanche and Delaware, all spoken on the same pitch as English, they could record in part, because Cherokee is a three-toned language.

Then they continued their search into Mexico, and there, near a little town then known as San Fernando, the younger men left Sequoyah resting in a cave in a bluff while they went into the town to purchase supplies. And there they found him when they came back. He had gone to sleep forever, probably in his seventieth year.

San Fernando has been abandoned, or its name has been changed now. The bluff has caved in across the front of the cave. Sequoyah's final resting place has never been discovered, nor should it be. This great American needs no marker over his grave.

The second Cherokee in the rotunda of the Oklahoma state capitol is William Penn Adair Rogers, known to much of the world in his own time as "ole Will." As the inscription over the door of Yale University's Harkness Library, a quotation from Rafael Sabatini's *Scaramouche*, has it, "He was born with a gift of laughter and a sense that the world was mad."

The event occurred on the ranch of his father, Clem V. Rogers, a part-Cherokee descendant of John Rogers, on November 4, 1879. The ranch actually was located near Oologah, but Will later claimed Claremore, I.T., as his home town, and it is at Claremore that Will is buried. His father was a stern disciplinarian, and his mother he once described as "an old-fashioned woman named Mary." He was the youngest child and only son in a family of five.

Will grew up in the Verdigris River country, and spent a good deal of his time exploring it, in spite of his father's attempts to send him to school. His first effort was at a girls' school when, at the age of four, he refused to be separated from his sister Sally (Mrs. McFadden), and became the only boy ever to attend the Young Ladies Academy at Vinita, I.T. Later he was sent to military academies, schools at Chelsea, I.T., and others, but the Dog Iron Ranch was home, and to it he returned. "Three years in McGuffey's Fourth reader and I knew more about it than McGuffey did," was his later description of his formal education.

To quiet young Will down and stay his wanderings, Clem Rogers finally gave his son the Dog Iron Ranch. By that time Will had developed a taste for country dances, roping contests and horse races, and had acquired a remarkable cow pony, Comanche. Somewhere he learned to fiddle, and he fiddled for some of the dances, but stock handling was his life and his love.

He met the Mulhall brothers from near Ponca City, and traveled with their show for a while, winning some contests and losing others. Somewhere along the line he met an

Arkansas girl, Betty Blake, and married her. She did not travel with the show, but it was a marriage of complete fidelity and fulfillment on either side. Neither of them wavered in devotion to the other.

At last the Mulhall show reached Madison Square Garden, in New York. By this time, Will had added exhibition roping to his act, and because he was nervous at first before large audiences, he chewed gum and commented on the news of the day as he worked. Florenz Ziegfeld "caught the act" one evening, and from that time on Will was part of the Ziegfeld *Follies*. Many of his bons mots date from that time. One was "One thing to be thankful for is that our soldiers can win wars faster than our diplomats can talk us into them," delivered at the time of the signing of the Treaty of Versailles in 1919. The most widely quoted was "I never met a man I didn't like," and it could truly be said that no one ever met Will who didn't like him.

Although Will lived and traveled among well-educated people, he studiously cultivated his "Oklahoma drawl" as part of his act. He wrote a newspaper column of political comment. He wrote a small book, *Ether and Me*, about his gallstone operation, which has become a collector's item. His column and book are proof enough that McGuffey stuck, at least. They are not written in the language of an uneducated man, but in that of a simple one.

Will Rogers was one of the earliest enthusiasts for flying. From the time he learned that you could travel by air as well as by land, he was up in the air most of the time, either flying himself or having as co-pilot another Oklahoman, Wiley Post.

When Ziegfeld died, Will accepted a motion picture offer, and moved, with his family—Clem, Mary and Will, Junior, and their mother—to a ranch outside Hollywood. He made it as nearly as possible a dream ranch house.

Will Rogers appeared in many pictures: *David Harum;* Homer Croy's *They Had to See Paris,* which tells of the experiences of a homesick Oklahoma family traveling in Europe (Croy had laid his story in Indiana, but to Will, home was Oklahoma); and, best-known of all, *A Connecticut Yankee at The Court of King Arthur,* from Mark Twain's immortal classic. In the Croy picture Will had started his custom of wearing two wrist watches, one set to Oklahoma time and one to the time of the place where he was. In *The Yankee* he determinedly placed the Oklahoma drawl ahead of the Connecticut version, and the result was long to be remembered.

President Calvin Coolidge had appointed Will "Ambassador to the World" from the United States, and the title was never withdrawn. Much of his traveling and flying time went into justifying it. He was a man of good will; it showed in his grin and his words, and no one at that particular time could better have represented the United States abroad. His death came in August 1935, at the age of fifty-six, when he and Post crashed in Frank Phillips' plane, the *Winnie Mae,* off Point Barrow, Alaska, trying to reach the Aleutian Islands.

People walked the streets of Oklahoma towns that day, muttering, "Not ole Will. NOT ole Will! And Wiley Post, too. That was a fine brave guy." Post had continued flying even after he lost the sight of one eye in World War I, and his trademark—long before Lord Hathaway—was an eye patch.

But it was for his generosities and kindnesses that Will was most remembered and will never be forgotten. During the early Depression, he maintained a staff of field nurses and social workers among the hill Cherokees of eastern Oklahoma. He helped to support Miss Alice Robertson, Oklahoma's first congresswoman, during her last, unhappy days. After his death, the Bureau of Indian Affairs discovered that it had to open almost thirty civil service positions to nurses and social workers to replace those Will had supported out of his own pocket.

How many generosities he did will never be known. More than just these. One of us remembers hearing of a Choctaw woman's selling him Indian baskets and his eagerness to buy and wryness about what he should do with them. But the baskets were made by Indians and the Indians had precious little to support them.

He was offered burial in Arlington National Cemetery, as an ambassador, but Betty chose to bring him back home to Claremore. The state of Oklahoma built a Will Rogers shrine, with archives, museum and memorabilia above the simple marble slab on which his name and Betty's are carved. Steps lead down to the rose garden surrounding it, and people stand with bowed heads above the grave. The bust Jo Davidson cast in bronze of him is in the main lobby of Oklahoma City's Airport, which is named for him, and Davidson's lifesize bronze faces the observer who enters the memorial. They are good likenesses, but they are static.

Charles Banks Wilson painted the man as he was. Rogers stands at the head of an air strip, a wind sock stretching above him, and the *Winnie Mae* waiting for him at the other end. He slouches slightly, like any old-time cowboy. His Stetson is creased and pushed to the back of his head; one hand, over whose arm is draped a light coat, is stuffed into the pocket of his jacket and the other pocket is thrust out by a rolled-up newspaper. Will, about to leave forever, and smiling a little about it. The genius who is Wilson saw the *man*, and his love for humanity, and so he showed him.

The third figure immortalized in the capitol rotunda is also Indian, but from a different tribe. Jim Thorpe was a Sauk and Fox, who was born near Yale, Oklahoma, in 1888. Unlike Rogers, who was privately educated when he went to school at all, Thorpe attended Carlisle Indian School, Carlisle, Pennsylvania.

This school was a remarkable experiment in Indian education, and was headed by a remarkable man, Richard Henry Pratt. It operated on what was called "the outing system." Six months of the year students lived and worked in the school; the other six months they were taken into homes, usually those of German Mennonites, in the surrounding country or in the cities.

Carlisle discipline was strict, and the school was noted for its athletic teams. Thorpe was only one of a group of highly trained and skilled athletes, but he outshone all of them. He could and did participate in any and all sports, but excelled in football and was captain of his team.

In 1912, Thorpe participated in the decathlon at the Olympic games in Stockholm. He won every event in which he took part. When someone asked Thorpe, after he had returned to Oklahoma, what he said when King Gustavus presented him with his medals, Thorpe replied, "I said, 'Thanks, King.'"

After the awards had been made, someone discovered that during one of his Carlisle summers Thorpe had played on a semiprofessional baseball team and did not qualify as an amateur athlete. The medals were returned to Stockholm and, in spite of many attempts to have them placed at Carlisle, or at the recently established Jim Thorpe Museum at Yale, Oklahoma, the Olympic Committee has so far retained them.

After he had been declared officially a professional athlete, Thorpe organized a professional football team, which many of his old Carlisle teammates joined. They traveled the United States, and went as far abroad as England, where they had to play exhibition games against each other, English soccer being as strange to them as American football was to the English. One of us has a New Jersey friend, a white man, who played on Thorpe's professional team.

Thorpe married a white woman. He died in Oklahoma in 1955 and was buried first there and then at Keokuk, Iowa, at his wife's insistence. This was a fearful breach of tribal etiquette, which decreed that after death a man returned to his own family in spirit, and had no further contact with his wife. "Everybody knew that woman was crazy when she married him," said one elderly Sauk and Fox woman at the time.

Thorpe was chosen as one of the four great Oklahomans because whatever he did in the field of athletics he did fairly and honestly. He represented the United States and Oklahoma for the world, and honestly did not know that he was not an amateur when he went to Stockholm. Nobody had bothered to tell him the difference. Wilson described his body, from photographs, as "perfection itself, the body of a Greek god." His detail drawings of arm and leg muscles show that Wilson spoke truly. As for the knees that were like "a bag of beans, they were so relaxed and so knit together," it is hard to believe that any man could have been so firmly built and still so relaxed.

The fourth "immortal," Robert Samuel Kerr, was born at Ada, in the Chickasaw Nation, September 11, 1896. The log cabin in which he was born is still standing and has been made a historical site. He once described his career as "from log cabin to the National Capital, and if I don't make it to the White House it won't be my fault."

Robert Kerr was the twelfth governor of Oklahoma, and the first who could be said to have been born in the state. He attended East Central Normal School at Ada, Oklahoma Baptist University at Shawnee, and the University of Oklahoma Law School at Norman. He taught school, practiced law and enlisted as a private in the United States Army in 1917. At the end of the war he was a second lieutenant of field artillery.

The beginning of his career was unfortunate. In four years he lost everything he had, including his first wife, and managed to run up debts amounting to ten thousand dollars. Then the luck turned; he married Grayce Breene, of Tulsa, and almost overnight because successful in the big business field of oil development.

In 1942, Kerr was elected governor, and in 1943, in January, he took the oath of office. He devoted much time and attention to the development of an improved school system and in reconstructing the Board of Regents for Higher Education. In 1946, Kerr was elected to the United States Senate, and he died in office on New Year's Day, 1963. The remainder of his term was served by the late J. Howard Edmondson, who resigned as governor to accept the appointment to the Senate.

Looking back, it would seem that Kerr singlehandedly accomplished the impossible—he changed the topography and climate of the entire state. Wilson has painted him standing by his senatorial desk, with maps and waterway charts displayed on the wall in the background. It is the portrait of a man of perception, ambition and drive. His drive exhausted his heart, and his ambition to construct an inland waterway from the Mississippi River to the town of Catoosa east of Tulsa was not achieved until seven years after his death, but there was no stopping him.

The Kerr ranch—he specialized in Black Angus cattle—near Poteau, in LeFlore County, southeastern Oklahoma, is now a museum and a recreation area.

Finally we come to a fifth Oklahoman whose portrait was not painted for the capitol rotunda and who was too controversial a figure for it to have hung there anyway—Alfalfa Bill Murray. He had been instrumental in getting the state constitution written and adopted. He served in both houses of the state legislature, and eventually became governor, as did his son, Johnston Murray.

But the young dandy, who courted Mary Alice Hearral in Tishomingo before statehood, underwent many changes in personality during his life. He was disgruntled by the reactionary attitude that followed World War I and vowed to turn his back on the United States forever. He gathered a group of colonists together, learned Spanish and taught it to everyone else, and departed for Bolivia. He held, with much justification, that the future of the world lay in the Latin-American countries.

Four years later Murray was back in Oklahoma. His money and that of his wife and followers was exhausted. Murray returned with two positive things: an Ecuadorian straw hat, of the kind most often called a "panama," and a taste for the maté tea grown in Bolivian highlands and until then almost unknown in the United States.

Undefeated, even by the difficulty of obtaining maté, Murray started his "pot likker and corn pone" campaign for governor. For those who grew up in other parts of the country, pot likker in the South and in Oklahoma is the liquid remaining in the pot after greens have been cooked, usually with bacon or "fat back" (salt pork), for hours. Whatever nutriment and vitamins the greens originally contained has dissolved in the pot likker. The substance is consumed by dipping in it pieces of corn pone—corn bread baked without flour, eggs or sugar, in a skillet, with bacon grease. This is dipped in the pot likker and the combination is eaten, usually with the fingers but sometimes with a spoon. It was the daily bread of many poor Southerners, and was probably responsible for as much pellagra and indigestion as any other combination.

Murray insisted that he was a poor man now, and traveled from town to town in an old Ford or on foot, making campaign speeches and consuming corn bread and pot likker with all and sundry. Just in case the local restaurants did not provide his chosen provender, he carried a Mason jar of pot likker and a paper bag of corn pone with him, and passed out samples.

The campaign was successful. Here was a man with whom the poor could identify, and there were many more poor Oklahomans than rich ones. Murray discarded his painfully acquired "book learning" and his truly exquisite Spanish to speak to the poor in their own language—the "seen and done" of the sharecropper he once had been. As the campaign progressed, he grew increasingly shabby. His hair straggled about his ears and his mustache drooped untrimmed around his mouth. He wore no coat, only an old brown sweater held together in front with a safety pin. People offered to clothe him more presentably, but not until he wore a hole in the seat of his britches and his wife insisted that he had to be presentable for his own inauguration did Bill Murray accept a new suit, a clean white shirt, shoes without holes in their soles and a necktie, all supplied by Will Rogers. He hung onto the old brown sweater and the safety pin, and wore them when he was working in his office.

During Murray's term in office, 1931-35, the Red River shifted its bed again, this time without the blessing or responsibility of the Army Corps of Engineers. The Oklahoma-Texas border had run through the middle of the stream bed. Texas claimed land that had once been part of Oklahoma, and started to build a toll bridge to establish the state's riparian rights. Murray charged to the fray like a Brahma bull coming out of its rodeo chute.

Corn pone and pot likker on hand to keep up his strength, he seated himself on a camp chair in the middle of the bridge span and defied the state of Texas to complete the bridge, charge the toll or move Alfalfa Bill. He called out the state National Guard to prove that he meant it. The matter was finally settled by the United States Supreme Court, which held that the line *still* ran through the middle of the river bed, neither state could build a toll bridge, and both must co-operate in the construction of a free one. It was a bitter day for Murray.

Still, just out of office in 1932, he began his "paper sack" campaign against Franklin D. Roosevelt. This must be called the low point in Murray's personal and moral life. Sack lunch in hand, he again crisscrossed the state, carrying on a single-handed and almost totally unsupported campaign for the Democratic nomination for President. He started a whispering campaign against Roosevelt which cost him many votes he might otherwise have had. The other candidate's lameness, said Murray, was not due to polio, as Roosevelt and his family and followers claimed, but to syphilis, contracted at Harvard. Murray held this up as an awful warning against anything but grass-roots education. Ivy towers were dens of vice and iniquity.

After his attempt at the presidency failed, Murray continued to deteriorate. He wrote his autobiography, in three thick volumes, and persuaded a commercial printing firm to publish it. He wandered the streets of Oklahoma City and Tulsa, loaded down with books, and tried to sell them to anyone and everyone he met. He had little success.

In 1955, after his wife died, and during his son Johnston Murray's term as governor, Alfalfa Bill was inducted into the Oklahoma Hall of Fame. He appeared for the festivities, on the arm of his daughter-in-law, the governor's wife, who was radiant in a formal evening gown, still wearing the old brown sweater, the safety pin and shoes with holes in them. To this attire he added a long brown knitted scarf, also secured with a giant safety pin. There were those in the audience who were unkind enough to whisper that at seventy-three he had reached his second childhood, and was held together with diaper pins.

Yet the young dandy who had come from Corsicana, Texas, in a top hat and tails, and had faded into blindness and senility after his wife's death should not be discounted. He was a man of terrific memory; his voice and manner of speaking were resonant and impressive, and he had enough personal magnetism to gather together his Bolivian colonists and persuade a foreign government to give them land for farming. A strange, contradictory man, his memory remains with many Oklahomans, and "ole Alfalfa Bill" is a man of many legends, like "ole Will Rogers."

12. Grant Foreman as a young man—at the time he came to Oklahoma.
    Courtesy of Oklahoma Historical Society.

13. William H. (Alfalfa Bill) Murray.
    Courtesy of Oklahoma Historical Society (Fred S. Barde Collection).

14. Early Cushing oil well blowing in.
Courtesy of Western History Collections, University of Oklahoma Library.

15. Barn and shed of a farm near Boise City, in the Panhandle, June 1938.
Courtesy of Western History Collections, University of Oklahoma Library.

16. A dust storm approaches Springfield. The storm reached city limits at 4:47 P.M., on May 21, 1937. Total darkness lasted about one-half hour.
Courtesy of Western History Collections, University of Oklahoma Library.

17. South Burleigh County District, August 1941, showing contour strip farming, alternating corn and small grain.
Courtesy of Western History Collections, University of Oklahoma Library.

CHAPTER 17

MISS ALICE

At the same time and in the same decade, a most proper lady rose to prominence. She was a *grande dame* in her own right, and someone once described her as "a chip off Plymouth Rock removed to Oklahoma." Alice Mary Robertson was a most contradictory person. People have idolized and idealized her, while at least one would-be biographer was so enraged by her letters as to give up the effort to write her life.

When John Held, Jr., and Frank Petty were creating their long-legged, short-haired, candy-box pretty, and oh, so naughty flappers, Miss Alice wore her sandy-white hair twisted in a bun on top of her head. She scorned make-up, and nobody ever knew the comparative lengths of her legs and her torso, because her skirts always descended in full sweeps to her ankles. She wore dresses of the same fashion as those affected by her mother, and she saw no reason to change her style.

In solidly, nostalgic, Democratic Muskogee, she was a Republican. Her family had always been opposed to slavery, and so was she—to every vestige of it. She was also opposed to women's suffrage, but she made her living from a cafeteria which she first opened as a club for working girls. She managed to be the second woman elected to the United States Congress and the first woman to preside over the House of Representatives. She was a schoolteacher who had never been able, because of poverty and family problems, to complete her college education.

Yes, Alice Mary Robertson, who was "Miss Alice" to the eastern half of Oklahoma, was a bundle of contradictions. It can hardly be held against her. She came of a family of missionaries, and she lived her life, as she said, "by the rule of God." And God help anyone who didn't agree with her.

Miss Alice's mother, Ann Eliza Worcester Robertson, was the child of missionaries who married a missionary. In her early childhood she played and studied with Indian children, for her father taught school in the intervals of circuit riding. Worcester, Massachusetts, had been named for the Worcester family, and so had Worcester College. Naturally, Ann Eliza used her playmates as sources of information. She learned Cherokee, Choctaw, Creek and Chickasaw. She also learned—her father saw to this—Latin, Greek, Italian and French. In her later days she taught herself German, but bemoaned the fact that although her two daughters were fair linguists in Indian tongues, her European languages were growing rusty, "for lack of someone with whom to use them."

The Worcester family moved to Indian Territory with the Cherokees, driving a covered wagon over that particular Trail of Tears. Loaded in the wagon, along with household equipment, clothing and chickens, went the Cherokee National Press and its fonts of Sequoyah type.

William Robertson, also a missionary, came out with the Creeks. It is easy to lose track of the men in this remarkable family, because of the achievements of the women. But there would have been no Cherokee National Press without Samuel Austin Worcester, Ann Eliza's father.

After Sequoyah's demonstration of the feasibility of writing Cherokee, the press and types were shipped from Boston to the Cherokee capital at New Echota, Georgia, and Samuel Austin Worcester, a missionary, was put in charge of training Cherokees in the use of the printed alphabet. The first book issued by the Cherokee National Press was *The Gospel According to St. Matthew*.

Worcester trained Elias Boudinot, a relative of John Rogers and a graduate of Dartmouth, to translate the Gospels and to set them in Cherokee type. The National Press had been in operation in Georgia for four years before the removal began, and Worcester and Boudinot traveled—press, types, and all —with the last group of Cherokees to leave the East.

The National Press was again set up in the basement of the national capitol at Tahlequah as soon as that building was completed, and continued in operation until statehood. It is now housed in the Oklahoma Historical Society Building in Oklahoma City.

And William Robertson rode his preaching circuit and was a doctor, lawyer, veterinarian, banker and general adviser to approximately ten thousand people in the Creek and Seminole nations. Eventually, probably at a church conference, his path crossed that of the Worcesters, and he met Ann Eliza.

They married. Somehow they managed to survive. In a day when a man might lie in his grave at the end of a windrow of wives, who had all died in childbearing, William and Ann

Eliza produced their three daughters, and neither of them ever had occasion to take a second mate. Survival was aided by the Presbyterian Board of Missions, which paid William a small salary. Sometimes William was paid—in kind—for some of his services. They secured horses, cows, chickens and planted a truck garden, so that the family was to a large extent self-supporting.

First Augusta, then Alice Mary and finally Grace were born. The Robertson family was never rich, but it never suffered. Its members gave what they had to share to their less fortunate neighbors. In between gardening, dressmaking, caring for her husband and their children, and keeping a house, Ann Eliza found time to continue her linguistic studies, and to compile a Creek grammar and dictionary. It was the first systematic study made of any Indian language.

After the Civil War, when the Robertson house was burned to the ground by night riders who disagreed with the family's anti-slavery stand, this study proved to be of value.

The Bureau of Ethnology (the word "American" was added to its title later) was organized as a branch of the Smithsonian Institution. The plan was to study the Indians, in a last, desperate hope that where warfare had failed to subdue the Plains tribes, knowledge and sweet reason might prevail. The fruits of understanding, it was hoped, would be peace on the borders and in the Southwest, where the Apaches and Zuñis were becoming a threat.

A one-armed Union veteran of Shiloh, Major John Wesley Powell, was appointed head of the Bureau. He was not only a good fighter but a scholarly man with an inquiring mind. Ann Eliza, when she read of the Bureau (she could never cut out a dress pattern lent her by a friend, said her second daughter, because she had to read both pieces of newspaper: the one she cut from and the one she cut), wrote to Major Powell and offered her services and those of her daughters as interpreters should anyone wish to study the tribes of the Indian Territory.

The major's reply was as prompt as any mail coming into the Territory could be in those days. He would like to see, if possible, some examples of the work the ladies were doing. Ann Eliza sent him a fair copy of her precious Creek grammar and dictionary. The rest is history. Ann Eliza was appointed a linguist on the Bureau staff; the greatest linguist, the major said, that the United States had produced. That was kudos enough, but more was to come. There was a small salary, and then the major prevailed on the administration of Elmira College, Elmira, New York, which Ann Eliza attended briefly before her marriage, to bestow on her the honorary degree of Doctor of Philosophy. It was the first such degree, honorary or otherwise, granted to a woman in the United States.

Elmira College influenced the Robertson family in many ways. Not only was it Ann Eliza's alma mater, but she was determined that at least one of her daughters should attend it and come home with an earned degree. The choice fell on Alice.

Pioneer days and their attendant hardships were taking their toll of the Robertson family. Augusta and Grace had married, and they and their husbands were undergoing the struggle their mother had known before them. William Robertson was ailing—increasingly feeble as cancer made its way through his body. Alice returned home at the end of her third year of college, and she never went back. The earned degree remained a dream. Once she said that the only day in her life when she wept aloud was the one that was to have been her graduation day. And then she went into the woods, alone, to cry her heart out.

William Robertson died, and his wife and second daughter lived on in the house he had built until it, too, was destroyed by fire. They moved into what had been formerly the cow barn, for a time. Then Alice gathered herself together, borrowed money from a wealthy Worcester relative, sent her mother to live with Augusta, and went to Washington, D.C. There, at nineteen, she became a clerk interpreter in the office of the Bureau of Indian Affairs. For a number of years she was not only the first, but the only, woman to hold such a position.

When the loan had been repaid, Miss Alice began to save for her return to Indian Territory. This time she had a job in the Muskogee office of the Bureau of Indian Affairs, and she staked her claim to land just outside town, on the southwest slope of Agency Hill, where the old Union Agency still stood, abandoned. Her mother returned to her, and the two women took first two, and then two more little Creek Indian girls—orphans—into their home to train and educate. They called the house Sawokla, a Creek Indian word which means The Gathering Place.

More and more Creek orphans materialized. They helped in the garden and house, and with the cows and chickens. In addition to learning to read and write, the children learned domestic science. But as more and more of them needed to be clothed and shod, it was evident that something had to be done to put the place on a firmer financial basis than the present hand-to-mouth scale of family living. Miss Alice organized a school and orphanage, later to be known as Minerva Place, from the name of one of the Worcester aunts, who had helped with finances. Ann Eliza probably found the name fitting for other reasons—the goddess of learning had spread her robe over Indian Territory.

Later the Presbyterian Board of Missions took over the school, and it became known as Henry Kendall College, for the president of the Board. This, in turn, became Tulsa University, and it was with much truth that Alice Robertson referred to herself as "the mother-in-law of Tulsa University." However, she and her mother continued to house and care for orphan girls in their own home.

The old missionary zeal blazed up. Once again Alice borrowed money from her Worcester relatives, and this time she took to the road. She went wherever people would pay, in donations to Minerva Place, to listen to her. She confessed in a letter to Augusta—the two sisters were always very close— that she suffered from butterflies before she spoke, but as soon as she was on her feet they flew away and she became a fluent and fascinating public speaker. Money came in, the second loan was repaid, and Minerva Place was secure for at least a year. Whereupon the Bureau of Indian Affairs built a Sequoyah Orphan Training School at Tahlequah, thirty miles away, and the need for Minerva Place was gone.

Alice returned the donations, as much as she could. Even then, Sawokla as she now called it again, represented a considerable investment in time, money and effort. It also produced a generous amount of garden produce in an area where garden produce was scarce. Alice began to fill the family wagon with fruits and vegetables, gathered early each morning, and drive into Muskogee to deliver produce to grocers, who were willing to pay well for fresh foods.

The Spanish-American War broke out, and trainloads of troops passed through Muskogee. Miss Alice met each one with "comfort kits," which she and her mother made. Each kit contained a small Bible, needles and thread, and other small creature comforts. As long as there was fruit to be given away, night or day, it went to the station, not the grocers. It is said that Miss Alice stormed San Juan Hill with her comfort kits. Certainly a great many of Theodore Roosevelt's Rough Riders came from eastern Oklahoma, cowboys and Indians being about equally mixed.

Ann Eliza passed to her well-earned reward soon after the war ended, and her daughter, born before the Civil War, in 1854, found herself a middle-aged woman, alone. For a time she taught in the schools of the Indian Bureau—as a matter of fact, she never ceased to teach. But teaching took her too much from her beloved Sawokla. She had filed her claim; now she took title, legally and in action. She opened a cafeteria—probably the first west of the Mississippi and south of St. Louis—in downtown Muskogee, and went into business for herself. It was one way of using up the surplus produce from Sawokla.

There was always a certain coyness about Alice Robertson. During her lecture tours she frequently wrote her sister about "all these distinguished people who come to listen to poor little me," and the image of the shy, retiring country schoolteacher, accurate or not, was one she clung to all her life.

She reached her apogee in her advertising for Sawokla Cafeteria, which she had originally begun as a club for working girls, and then opened to the public. She wrote, for instance:

> We do not find "business as usual" any better than usual. . . . Lots of hot soup today, and catfish, fried brown. Sweet potatoes getting sweeter every day; pole beans, boiled

with bacon in the pot; corn bread, made from white meal; buttermilk, cherry pie.

And again!

> Watermelons better every day. Fried chicken extra good tonight . . . we are not neglecting our customers.

This was in 1920, when she had declared of herself, "I am a Christian. I am an American. I am a Republican." And became a candidate for Congress.

Alice Robertson had met Theodore Roosevelt on one of her lecture tours, and deeply admired him. Just as deeply she deplored Woodrow Wilson, for so many reasons that they cannot be stated here. During World War I she organized the equivalent of an American Red Cross canteen corps, with her friends. Again they met every troop train that passed through Muskogee, at whatever hour. Coffee, food and—concession to the world around her, whatever her personal feeling in the matter of smoking might be—cigarettes were handed up to reaching hands. No serviceman or his family could buy a meal at Sawokla Cafeteria. No woman worked harder or more tirelessly than Alice Mary Robertson.

In announcing herself as a candidate for Congress, she could not help observing that "many came to the cafeteria, not to eat, but, to look at the only woman candidate for office." She conducted a homey, folksy campaign, never going far from home, about on a par with her cafeteria advertisements. From a fifty-year perspective, one sees that she missed her calling. Today's Madison Avenue would have rejoiced in her.

In the Republican landslide of 1920 she was elected. There is little doubt that even in the 1968 landslide she might have been less successful. Women's lib would never have tolerated a woman who stood squarely—oh, how squarely—on her own two feet, ran "on the issues and her character" and took and gave no quarter. She never claimed equality with men. She had spoken out against women's suffrage. But when she was elected she returned to Washington. The proudest day of her legislative career was when she stood, holding the gavel, beside "Uncle Joe" Cannon, Speaker of the House, and presided over the august body.

Alice Robertson opposed many issues besides women's suffrage which she might have been expected to support. She turned her thumbs down on veterans' bonuses and even pensions; the men had volunteered to fight; they had not been drafted, and should not be rewarded in money for doing what was simply their duty.

Predictably, she fought against every movement to do away with the prohibition against alcoholic beverages. "Wine is a mocker and strong drink is raging" she frequently reminded her opponents. This did not endear her to many people in eastern Oklahoma.

Alice Robertson's second campaign for Congress in 1922 failed dismally, and she returned to Muskogee, defeated. Her health was beginning to fail. Sawokla had burned to the ground, and the cafeteria had to be sold to provide funds for living. She was too old to take a job, but she could begin to gather together the letters and mementos of a literarily prolific family and put them in order for the writing of history.

The last years were dim ones. One of us, working at her first job as a library cataloguer, was assigned, as the youngest member of the staff, to help Miss Alice when she wanted reference material. Miss Alice's office was in the basement of the library, but she was provided with a bell and when she wanted something she rang it—loud and clear. From the cataloguing room in the second story back to the front basement meant three flights of steep stairs, and they were to be negotiated—on the double.

Her money was exhausted. Will Rogers, as he did many times for many people, stepped in to save the day. As it became more evident that cancer was having its way with her as it had with her father, Lew Wentz, of Ponca City, Will Rogers' friend, another art collecting oil millionaire, helped Will establish her in the Will Rogers Hotel in Claremore. Here it was hoped that the readily accessible mineral waters —the hotel was built over a radioactive spring—would at least relieve her pain. Wentz was not a personal friend of Miss Alice's, but a man who acted from a sense of duty. No one who had contributed as much to Oklahoma as Alice Robertson should die in need. In 1932, the flag on the Muskogee Federal Building was lowered to half-staff in recognition of the passing of a great woman.

It is not easy to analyze Alice Mary Robertson. In her own town, in her own day, she was laughed at and derided for her standards and her unflinching courage. But when the Five Civilized Tribes Museum opened on the crest of Agency Hill, beside the Veterans' Hospital, which Miss Alice had fought to have built, the Museum Board of Trustees voted unanimously to establish an Alice Mary Robertson Room, furnished as nearly as possible with the shabby remnants she had saved from Sawokla and reproducing the living room her family and friends had known.

She had friends—many friends. Few of them were intimate, except her sister, Augusta. She preferred to maintain friendship by correspondence, and her letters could be warm. More often they were scorching.

Say, with Freudian glibness, that she was jealous of her mother's scholarship and of her sisters' happy married lives and their children. Say she resented being the man of the family, and envied her father's comparative freedom when he rode circuit. Say rather that she was an enigma and a contradiction, and so she remains.

She was not a lovable woman. She gave greatly of herself, but it is doubtful that she knew how to accept. Instead she bristled. But she set out to do things—and she did them.

CHAPTER 18

DR. FOREMAN AND THE WPA

Unlike Miss Alice Robertson, who was born at Tuskahoma Mission, Creek Nation, in 1854, Grant Foreman could not be called a native Oklahoman. He was born in Detroit, Illinois (no, this is not a mistake in states; we looked it up), in 1869, attended the University of Michigan Law School, and, in 1899, he reversed Lochinvar's directions and went into the West at least as far west as Muskogee, Indian Territory.

For four years he was a field worker with the Dawes Commission. This was a commission established to allot the Indians' lands and wind up the national affairs of the Five Civilized Tribes before statehood was enacted. "Nations within a nation" must now become "tribes."

The commission was known by other names, as chairmen succeeded each other, but Henry Dawes was a sticker, and the commission is best known by his name.

In Muskogee, Grant Foreman met Judge Robert Thomas, and the two men became friends. The young field worker was invited to the Thomas home, where he met Mrs. Thomas,

Robert Thomas, Junior, and the reigning belle and heiress of Muskogee, Carolyn Thomas. Why Miss Thomas was still unmarried at an age when her contemporaries, in many cases, were well along with raising families, nobody knows. She was certainly popular and she never lacked for beaux. There may have been a touch of the bluestocking about her, even then, and certainly her father would have been hard to convince that any man in Muskogee was good enough for his Carolyn.

She was sweet, she was a great beauty, and after her mother's death she became a noted and gracious hostess. Grant Foreman lost his heart, and so, almost immediately, did Carolyn. Foreman resigned from his job as field worker to become Judge Thomas' law partner. Two years later, in 1905, the couple was married in Grace Episcopal Church. At the judge's request they shared his home. After the judge was killed in a prison uprising he was trying to control at the state penitentiary in McAlester, the Foremans continued to occupy the house which is now a state monument and is known as "The Thomas-Foreman Home." It stands at 1419 West Okmulgee Street, Muskogee, in one of the loveliest gardens in a city of beautiful gardens. Grant Foreman to the end of his days boasted that he was the only man to plant and maintain a sugar maple tree that far south.

Occupy the house the Foremans certainly did. Mrs. Rella Looney, who was for many years their secretary, and is now archivist, Indian Archives Division of the Oklahoma Historical Society, has said that she never opened the hall closet to hang up her coat without being ready to duck if a cascade of papers, books, etc. descended unexpectedly. Every inch of available space was taken up with written or printed matter.

The Foremans never took anything but working vacations. They traveled widely in this country and abroad, and Carolyn once counted 113 institutions, libraries, etc., where they had toiled through documents and records. When they were not traveling, even while Dr. Foreman continued his law practice, they were beginning to write. In 1926, Grant Foreman's *Pioneer Days in the Early Southwest* was published by the A. H. Clark Company (Cleveland, Ohio), and a solid, steady scholarly output of books began. They were not as readable —except for persons with minds as analytical as Grant Foreman's—as his wife's, but they represented a tremendous contribution to knowledge of a previously neglected period and place.

More than the sugar maple grew in the garden, There were roses, wisteria, honey locust trees and a host of annuals. It was a haven for birds, and the Foremans made a morning ritual of bird feeding. Indeed, the birds were so abundant that it was necessary to keep special hats available for garden sitting.

After resigning from his law practice, Grant Foreman concentrated even more intently on his studies. He was becoming aware that there was work in the history of the Southwest for several lifetimes, and that he was not getting any younger. The Depression had set in with the stock market crash of 1929, but those were still only words to most Oklahomans.

Foreman began collecting data on his own. As one after another of the state's distinguished citizens passed into history, he swooped, with the true zeal of the pack-rat collector, on their bewildered families and scooped up all the paper he could get his hands on. His own statement on the subject was to the effect that "To follow a clue to its lair of an elusive historical event; to capture and make it fast, and to make it my own, brings a glow of satisfaction I would not yield to any big game hunter."

Nor did he. When the Oklahoma Historical Society building was constructed, he insisted that a room to house the papers be set aside. One of the twenty-four directors of the Society, and after he received his honorary doctorate from his alma mater, director emeritus for life, he transferred his assortment of documents to Oklahoma City, trained and installed Mrs. Looney as archivist, and made her appointment conditional on her being the *only* archivist the state should have as long as she lived and wanted to keep on working. Mrs. Looney started on the job in 1929, and is still going strong.

In fact, if he had done nothing else in his lifetime and he did a great many important things Grant Foreman would deserve a star in his crown for Mrs. Looney. More than any of the researchers who work in her crowded office, she knows the history of all of Oklahoma and has known many of its prominent men. She loved and worked well with Dr. Foreman, and she adored Mrs. Foreman and named her own daughter Carolyn. She is truly dedicated to her work, and carrying on the Foreman researches is an act of devotion for Rella Looney, who has never in her modest quiet life received the recognition she deserves. Without her, the history of the western frontier could probably never be written.

The Depression and New Deal of the 1930s hit western Oklahoma simultaneously with a ten-year drought. Whatever Mr. Steinbeck may have thought from his seclusion on the coast, Sallisaw, where he laid the opening scenes of *The Grapes of Wrath*, was a good three hundred miles east of the actual dust bowl.

The novel annoyed a good many Oklahomans, among them Dr. Foreman, who was a man of an accurate, legal turn of mind. He set out to correct Mr. Steinbeck's errors in geography, pronunciation and, above all, in the use of the dirty word "Okie" as applied to the citizens of the Sooner state.

After all, the University of Oklahoma's fight song, roared to the tune of Yale's "Boola Boola," has as its refrain "Boomer, Sooner, Boomer, Sooner." Nobody could foresee the day when the second Republican governor elected in the state's history would put out "Okie" pins, bumper stickers and other miscellaneous objects to "boost" the state. The time to stop that nonsense was before it started. Dr. Foreman was the man to do it, and he very nearly did.

The Blue Eagle was flying in store windows as a symbol of voluntary price controls. Dr. Foreman betook himself to Oklahoma City, and there he and Mr. Cunningham conferred on the problems of employment of unskilled labor, highly skilled labor and professional people. Dr. Foreman wisely utilized the information Mr. Cunningham provided and developed projects from which the state's citizens would benefit for years to come.

Dr. Foreman organized a project for the collection of data on Oklahoma history. It was long before the day of portable tape recorders, so his people gathered documents or recorded interviews with pencil and paper. Among them they accumulated a truly astounding record for a state so young.

Miss Eula Fullerton was summoned from her job as dean of women at Northeastern Oklahoma Teachers' College, at Tahlequah, and put in charge of women's projects with particular emphasis on those which could and would employ Indian women. Mrs. Eula Looney, a Chickasaw, co-operated with the Bureau of Indian Affairs and the Indian Arts and Crafts Board of the Department of the Interior to establish arts and crafts projects for Indian women all over the state. Canning, preserving and distribution of food products were more directly Miss Fullerton's affairs.

The Civilian Conservation Corps came into existence,

sheltering men under twenty-one (and quite a few who were older) in abandoned army barracks. The CCC built fire roads instead of trails through eastern Oklahoma forests, paved new roads and built more dams.

Everywhere that something was going on you could find Dr. Foreman. Did the construction of a dam threaten an archaeological site? The one-man Department of Anthropology, with all available University of Oklahoma students who could be interested in that recondite subject, went to work excavating it, with WPA labor manning the shovels and the students following through to the fine work with trowels and brushes. Was another dam going to flood a stand of virgin timber: walnut, pecan, wild cherry, juniper? Quick with the tools! The wood could be cut, split and used for furniture making at Indian Service schools after it had seasoned.

It was the first salvage archaeology work in the United States, although nobody called it that at the time. And it all stemmed—along with a list of eighteen scholarly works—from the fertile brain of Dr. Foreman. He knew everybody in the state, and everybody knew him. He could find the men with money to sponsor projects that would receive matching federal funds.

Every museum in the state, and some new ones that were started as WPA projects themselves, contributed to and benefited from this work. There was nothing much anybody could do about the dust bowl west of the Cross Timbers, but eastern Oklahoma, rich in logwoods as well as archaeology, became a changed and flourishing place. In the beginning, the average cash income of a Choctaw family in eastern Oklahoma was $49.50. Now it is, in spite of current inflation, $1,250 by the most reliable figure available. Much of the increase has come from skills learned on WPA projects, and taught to sons and daughters as the first students aged and could no longer carry on the hard physical work of their own youth.

Dr. Foreman died in 1953 in the White House in Muskogee. Carolyn Thomas Foreman survived him, still working, still the gracious hostess, until 1967, when she died at the age of ninety-five. The house rightfully has been declared a historic site, and is under the protection of the Oklahoma Historical Society. Mrs. William Bigelow Neergaard, Mrs. Foreman's niece and only heir, deeded it to the Society in 1969.

CHAPTER 19

THOSE DAMN DAMS

How the Army Corps of Engineers got into the picture during WPA days, nobody can quite remember. Probably Max Cunningham—again! Any engineer was a friend of his, and any engineer should be given the right to build whatever he pleased, Army or civilian.

In this case, "The engineers with hairy ears, whose pants were leather britches," decided that the dust bowl drought might be relieved by construction of windbreaks and farm ponds. They chose native plants for the windbreaks: cedar, locust and *bois d'arc*. These had a better chance of taking hold than plants brought from other areas.

Then came the farm ponds. "Erosion checks" were piled up in the gullies and small canyons. The checks were composed of abandoned automobiles, windbreak trees that had not survived after all, boulders, sand and gravel. They were built with WPA labor, and any farmer who was willing to contribute land might have one, for the erosion checks were inexpensive to build.

The combination of windbreaks and small farm ponds was a blessing to western Oklahoma. What little water did fall was accumulated in the ponds, and the stock began to prosper again. County Demonstration Agents urged that the land be resown with the native grama, bluestem, johnson, and buffalo grass, and pastures began to replace blown-out wheat fields and corn acreages. Children in western Oklahoma learned to swim, a luxury previously denied to most of them.

But then the Army Corps of Engineers began to go hog-wild. The Tennessee Valley Authority was flourishing in the poverty areas of the southern Appalachians, providing not only water but electric power from Muscle Shoals, Pickwick, Hiwassee and other dams. Industry was coming into the area. Why wouldn't the same thing work in western Oklahoma? Only because the streams there were largely muddy and shallow and ran with brackish water. Well, then, there was eastern Oklahoma. The Grand River Dam Authority came into being.

The Grand River rises in Missouri and flows across northeastern Oklahoma to a confluence with the Illinois and Arkansas rivers. These are good, clear, steadily flowing rivers, with a strong tendency to get out of hand during their spring and autumn floods. Damming them would control the floods, furnish sources of power, water, and recreation on the resulting lakes, and eventually open the waterway to the Mississippi. With the blessing of most county commissioners, the engineers, in the local phraseology, "went ahead on."

Oklahoma City's source of public water supply came from Lake Overholser, created by damming the Canadian River. As the city grew, Lake Overholser proved insufficient as a source of city water. It had never been a source of hydroelectric power, because the Canadian did not flow strongly enough.

Water rationing in Oklahoma City was of frequent occurrence, especially in drought years.

So the Canadian was dammed again, farther upstream, and Lake Heffner was created. Beaver River, in the Oklahoma Panhandle, was dammed to make Fort Supply and Canton reservoirs. Since water has an urgency to run downhill, the process of supplying Oklahoma City was simple. When one lake got low, the floodgates of the next above it were opened, and nature took its course. The water filled the lower lake, and the city again drew its water supply.

However, although these dams date from the 1930s, it is still necessary to boil drinking water at certain times of the year in central Oklahoma. By some complicated process of physics, the water in a lake literally "turns over," spewing up dead fish and active algae in profusion. Sometimes the water from a lake that has just turned over runs into one that has not, with sad results for housewives. Occasionally not only drinking, but laundry water must be boiled before it can be used without assaulting the nose.

Again these inconveniences must be weighed against the advantages of a more abundant and steady supply of water. The trees planted along the lake shores, whether by nature or by man, provide pleasant picnicking and camping areas. Boating and water skiing, once something most Oklahomans saw only in the movies, have become major sports. Marinas have been built in the most unlikely places; it is always astonishing to drive across the short-grass country and suddenly be confronted with a lake and everything that goes with it.

Fishing has become not only a sport, but the raising of fish in state-owned hatcheries, to be released in the state's lakes, has improved the quantity and variety of fish available.

Oklahomans—some of them—have even learned to eat fish and like it.

Boatbuilding is a major industry, all over Oklahoma. On weekends the roads are dense with boatowners towing their fiber-glass craft behind the family cars, headed for the lakes.

Lake Texhoma, straddling Oklahoma and Texas in the southeast, has provided an unequaled opportunity for ecology study for students from both states. Not only fish and other aquatic animals are studied: herpetology flourishes, and so does the study of prairie wildlife, all in one place.

Most of all, the lakes have changed the climate of Oklahoma. The old saying "If you don't like the weather, wait a minute, it'll change" is no longer applicable. There is more moisture in the air; different plants grow more freely, and from being a part of the Great American Desert western Oklahoma in particular has developed into only a semiarid region. Some cloud seeding still is necessary to bring moisture to the plains, and legislation has been enacted to regulate and control it. Cattle from the bone-dry Panhandle were shipped to Australia for fattening and sale in September 1971, as well as vice-versa. But that was only temporary. The clouds have been seeded and the rains have fallen again.

Only one industry has failed to benefit from the construction of dams. The climate is now too damp to provide a refuge for tubercular and arthritic patients. Oklahoma's loss has been Arizona's gain, as the doctors send their patients ever westward.

CHAPTER 20

JOHNNY SCHMOKER'S COLONY

President Grant inaugurated his "peace policy" toward the Indians in 1872, and to make sure it remained peaceful he put members of the Society of Friends, or Quakers, in charge of as many Indian agencies as possible. Brinton Darlington, who was one of them, was assigned to build an agency and school south of Fort Reno, in a bend of the Canadian River. The place was soon named Darlington. It was to administer the affairs of the southern bands of the Cheyenne and Arapaho Indians.

Cheyennes and Arapahos are linguistically related; members of the great Algonquian family of Indian languages. Both shared in the horse culture of the Plains Indians. They are handsome groups of people, and their women are fine crafts workers. In temperament they differ considerably; Cheyennes are at once withdrawn, aggressive and mystic, while the Arapahos, with plenty of their own mysticism, it is true, are more outgoing and less resentful of strangers. The Cheyennes split, and one group left the heat and muddy water of Darlington Agency to go back to the wooded mountains and the clear streams of Montana. That tragic story has been told many times. The Arapahos stayed about where they were, within reach of Darlington Agency.

When it was apparent that enough Indians would stay within reach, Brinton Darlington decided to begin construction of a permanent school and office buildings. But when he inquired among eager, zealous Quakers who formed his staff, he found that not one of them knew anything about the construction of frame or brick buildings. A builder must be imported from the East.

By this time another Quaker, John D. Miles, had taken over the Darlington Agency. The head farmer, Joshua Trueblood, told Miles he knew a man living in New Malden, Kansas, who could turn his hand to anything. John Homer Seger, born in Ohio of British and Dutch parents, responded to a letter from the agent, and came to Darlington.

Lumber and bricks were non-existent in that part of Oklahoma Territory. Construction materials had to be shipped from the railhead at Wichita, Kansas, 150 miles of wagon road across the short-grass country. The materials were laboriously transported to the agency, and unloaded and piled there, ready for Seger and his crew—he was to enlist as many Indians as he could—to begin work.

About that time a band of Cheyennes came in from their summer hunt, and set up camp between the agency and the river. Firewood was scarce, and the women, in a hurry to get their families fed, swooped down on the neatly stacked lumber, ignoring the fragments of the older school, which were scattered about the site.

The agency employees were gathered at dinner in the communal dining room of their quarters when the depredation began, full in their view. Seger was outraged. He leaped up from the table and started for the door. In vain did Miles, Trueblood and the rest try to hold him back. The Quakers were frankly afraid of being massacred.

Seger was no Quaker. With the light of battle in his eye, he dashed outside, jumped on the woodpile, and began telling the Cheyennes just what he thought of them. Whenever a woman picked up a stick of new lumber, he took it from her, gently but firmly, and substituted a piece of scrap wood. And all the time, being no more a Cheyenne than he was a Quaker, he jumped up and down and yelled. As people do when speaking to those whose language is foreign to them, Seger yelled louder and louder, and finally noise and action convinced the Cheyennes that he wanted the new lumber *to stay right where it was.* Defeated and grumbling, the women withdrew, and cooked their supper over fires of old wood.

When the construction of the permanent agency, quarters and school were completed, Seger had learned that Cheyennes and Arapahos simply would not work together. He had also earned himself the name "Johnny Schmoker." Unlike the rest of the staff, who were strict-rule Quakers, Seger smoked— big black cigars, even more potent than pipes stuffed with Indian tobacco. He was also in the habit of crooning, while he worked, an old German folksong with the refrain *"Johnny Schmoker, Johnny Schmoker, Ich kann spiele, Ich kann spiele, Ich kann spiele, Meine Kleine Dudelsack."* The Indians never afterward called him anything but Johnny Schmoker, even after he had learned to speak Arapaho and earned himself another and more dignified Indian name.

After considerable argument, discussion and writing back and forth to Washington, Seger was granted permission to take a group of the more "progressive" Arapahos south of

Darlington, and to found a school, build houses, establish a church (Dutch Reformed, it need hardly be said) between the Canadian and Washita rivers.

It has become the custom to refer to the Indians who made up Seger's Colony, as it was called, as "coffee coolers," or agency hangers-on. As a matter of fact they were not. The Indians certainly did not disdain coffee or doughnuts, or many other white man's foods, it is true. But they saw the handwriting on the wall. It was plain that the whites had come to stay. Since they couldn't lick 'em, the Arapahos, especially, jined them.

It was to the school that Mary Little Bear and Minnie Bear ran away from the Cheyenne Sun Dance Camp, near the settlement that is now Watonga, Oklahoma. They were ten and eleven years old and determined to learn the white man's ways. Both were half-orphans and Mary Little Bear suffered the additional handicap of being half-white. Her mother's brother was a Sun Dance chief, her brother was being trained to succeed him, and Mary felt herself displaced —disoriented from Cheyenne life. Minnie was simply ambitious. She wanted to learn, to get a job and make money like a white schoolteacher.

When he was convinced that the two girls were in earnest, Seger took them in and put them to work; at first in the school laundry. Later he moved Mary to the sewing room and Minnie stayed in the laundry. Somehow, they became acquainted with two Caddo boys, cousins, Robert Cross and James Inkanish.

Both girls were trained in the Episcopal faith by Joshua Givvens, a Kiowa, one of the first Carlisle School graduates and the only positively known Episcopalian ever to exist in the Kiowa tribe. In fact, he was an ordained priest, and alternated his Sunday services with the Reverend F. H. Wright, a Dutch Reformed minister. The girls were ecumenically inclined, however, and when they married their Caddoes it was in the Dutch Reformed Church Seger had succeeded in establishing. Mr. Givvens was dead, and Rev. Wright officiated at the weddings.

Colony was a lovely spot. Unlike Darlington, which was out on the bald open prairie, it lay in the folds of red sandstone hills, which had eroded to make rich bottom land soil. There were trees; employees lived in white frame houses, and similar houses were constructed for those Indians who would live in them. The school and dormitories were of red brick. The little Dutch Reformed Church was built of yellow sandstone.

It was the church that really brought Colony its greatest fame. It urged Indian women to help their families by making and selling the fine quillwork and beadwork for which they were famous. Reese Kincaide, who came as a young minister from the Lake Mohonk Conference, was put in charge of both the church and the beadwork. There he stayed until a few years before his death, when he moved building and contents to a location east of Clinton, facing Highway 66, in hope of better sales.

It is difficult to estimate the effect of Seger and Kincaide on Oklahoman Indian arts and crafts. Kincaide compiled a monumental collection of Indian designs, taken from the work of tribes in all parts of the United States. He and Seger were both small men, but they were hard workers who worked well together.

The Mohonk Lodge beadwork became internationally famous, and orders came in from all over the world. Far from leaving the women to their own creative devices, Kincaide issued to a worker the design she was to follow; the material from which moccasins, handbags or anything else was to be made, and the precise number of beads in the correct colors to be used. These were charged to the worker, and when she returned the finished object she was credited and also paid an amount equal to half the value of the materials. The Mohonk Lodge sold the work for twice the amount invested in a piece, and maintained itself, the church and the minister, without, however, making much profit. Only one other non-Indian person has ever been said by the Cheyennes to measure moccasins so exactly, before cutting, as Reese Kincaide.

Colony was surrounded by gardens and corn fields, all well tended. There were chicken runs and pastures for cattle and horses. A donkey cart in charge of a team of older boys policed the grounds, thus inculcating, it was hoped, a love of cleanliness (Indian camps of the old days had never been dirty) and a knowledge of management of draft animals. The girls were taught to gather eggs and set the hens to hatch chicks. The boys were taught to feed and groom the livestock, and to milk. All were *made to drink the milk.* This was a terrible breach of Plains Indian mores, where only nursing babies ever swallowed the stuff, but Seger came from dairy country and milk went down, even down the throats of eighteen-year-old boys, who by their own standards were grown men and ready for warfare.

Seger lived to write his memoirs, *Early Days Among the Cheyenne & Arapaho Indians,* which were edited by the late Walter Stanley Campbell (Stanley Vestal), and published in pamphlet form in 1924. Later, Campbell added more material he had gathered from Seger, and the book was reissued in hard cover by the University of Oklahoma Press in

1934. The book is still as readable today as when it was first written. It has never gone out of print.

The school was taken over by the Bureau of Indian Affairs, and was finally closed in 1942, when integration of Indian students into public schools became an established government policy for all who were not orphans or the victims of broken homes. Kincaide moved to his new location on the highway, and shortly afterward was killed in an automobile accident. His building still stands, and is operated by N. B. Moore, a Creek.

The Seger school was gutted beyond repair by arson, after several abortive attempts, on September 6, 1971. It had just been declared a national historic site and placed in the care of the Oklahoma Historical Society. As one member of the committee in charge of historic sites for the state observed, "Oh, well, it's even more impressive now than it used to be. You just can't beat a grand old ruin for a tourist attraction!"

Perhaps the tourist attraction will bring back to Colony some of the life and bustle it once had. Now it is almost a ghost town. Robert and Minnie Cross still live in their little white frame house across from the school grounds, which was assigned to them when Robert graduated and went to work for the school. James and Mary Inkanish moved to Anadarko, where in the fullness of time they died. Nobody who ever knew either one of them will soon forget them.

Once, after Mary Inkanish was widowed, we took her to Colony to see her school friend, Minnie Cross. The two women had become fluent in their own brand of English in speaking to their husbands. As the afternoon wore on, more and more Cheyenne words came tumbling out, until no other language was spoken that day. We returned Mrs. Inkanish to her home in Anadarko in the early dusk. "Hah-ho!" (thank you) she said, for she had not yet been able to shift back to English.

Ghost town or not, Colony comes to life on Labor Day weekends for the Cheyenne powwow. Then beads and feathers are seen and pounding drums are heard. Songs are sung in many Indian languages. Memories stir and blend, and one perceives the blending of color and design that Reese Kincaide managed to bring about. No purist anthropologist, he.

CHAPTER 21

THEY CAME AND THEY STAYED

Oklahoma came into being at a time of world-wide financial crisis—the great time of bank closings and stock exchange crashes in 1890 came on the heels of the first land opening.

It was also the beginning of the great European Jewish tragedies that began with pogroms in Russia, Poland and Hungary, and terminated in genocide in Germany in the 1930s. Jews came to America from all over Europe. The great majority of them stayed in the eastern states, where they prospered or not, according to their own gifts. Some of them came West.

Some of these "forgotten pioneers" have been immortalized by Edna Ferber, Harry Golden, and Oklahoma's own Lewis Meyer. Both Miss Ferber and Mr. Meyer concentrated on Oklahoma; Mr. Golden has written of the pack peddlers of the southeastern United States, and Alice Marriott of those of the Southwest. Still, there are stories to be told.

There is, for instance, the story of Jacob B. Tingley and his daughter, Irma. Jake got as far as Anadarko, in southwestern Oklahoma, about 1900. In those days Anadarko consisted of two parallel streets, one of them, Main Street, paved. Broadway, which became known later as "the Indian Main Street," was not, nor were the north and south grid streets that crisscrossed the principal ones, which ran east and west. There were false-front buildings, some of brick and some of frame. Riverside Indian School, and the old Wichita Agency (which also served the Caddoes, Delawares, Kiowas, Comanches and Apaches, who were native to the area or had been removed there) were north of town. Anadarko itself, even into the 1930s, looked a little too much like the set of a Western movie to be believed.

From Anadarko Jake traveled through the surrounding Indian country, sometimes with a pack on his back, sometimes in a wagon. He traded household utensils and notions to Indian and non-Indian housewives; farm tools to their husbands. He made a modest stake, but not enough to achieve his ambition, which was to open a store. Then the biggest gambler and the most notorious saloonkeeper in still-wet Oklahoma Territory bet his wad on Jake.

He really gambled on Jake *and* his brother, but not even one who knew him well remembers what the brother's name was. He was "Jake's brother" to one and all, and so he remained.

Now Jake began to branch out. Allotments and Indian unemployment went hand-in-hand in that part of Oklahoma. Jake began to take in beadwork, featherwork, shawls and silver in trade from the Indians. He kept a supply of crafts materials on hand, and, like Reese Kincaide at Mohonk Lodge, he furnished supplies to Indian workers. Like Kincaide, too, he had an unerring eye for the rare and the beautiful. Again like Kincaide, Jake did not sell all his finest specimens, but kept them for his own pleasure.

Just how much of Anadarko Jake owned when he died is a question. He had prospered, he had bought real estate, he had married and produced children. Certainly none of Jake's family ever went wanting.

Once fire swept through his store, destroying many of his treasures. Careless volunteer firemen swept cascades of water over others. Jake, shaken and sorrowing, pulled himself together, procured new fixtures for his store, and packed away the damaged articles that he thought might still be salvageable in trunks in a back room.

His brother died a few years later, and Jake was much alone until his youngest daughter, Irma, moved from Tulsa to join him. Irma learned little Kiowa or Comanche, although her father spoke both fluently, with some Caddo and Delaware thrown in for good measure. He was the first adult white man to learn the five-toned Kiowa language since James Mooney, an ethnologist from the Smithsonian Institution, who worked with the tribe in the 1890s. Both were fluent in Indian sign language.

Jake was more Indian than the Indians. They loved and trusted him. His religion was never questioned; He attended powwows, peyote meetings, the Baptist church, and the temple in Lawton (when he could get away) impartially. He was just Jake, and a good guy; a member of the community. No Indian counted a trip to Anadarko complete without a stopover at Jake's.

Anadarko was changing with the times. Most of the streets were paved now. The false fronts on the buildings had been replaced with other false fronts—most of them modeled on *House and Garden*. There was no parking in the center of the street any more, and there were two decent places to eat. The old Indian Agency had been moved into the new downtown Federal Building, although Riverside School remained in its old location northwest of town. The decrepit buildings of the old Agency were hidden by the city fathers behind rows of cedar trees, where they quietly fell apart. The American Indian Exposition had replaced the one-day Indian Fair at the county fair grounds and was negotiating for the old Agency property, in order to provide a year-round tourist attraction. Meantime, the Chamber of Commerce went ahead with its own plans for the same kind of thing—Indian City, U.S.A., on a hill south of Anadarko.

About this time it was discovered that in some of his wall cases and back-room trunks Jake kept objects any museum might desire. Several did. If you got there early enough in the morning, so that you were the first customer of the day, you could come away with all sorts of goodies. The Indian Arts and Crafts Board of the Department of the Interior bought from Jake specimens to be used as models in the WPA arts and crafts program, thus further confusing the picture for ethnological purists.

When the Board opened a museum in Anadarko its first director, Royal Hassrick, spent more time in Jake's store than he did in his office. And learned more, he said, than he had at the University of Pennsylvania in his anthropology courses,

Probably the most persistent museum customer of all was the late great Frederic Douglas of the Denver Art Museum. Dr. Douglas was devoted to the accumulation of what he called "synoptic series" of specimens. If he had one beaded peyote fan, he wanted one from each tribe that made beaded peyote fans. He wanted fans in every design and color that any Indians used; he wanted the beaded rattles that matched the fans. Dr. Douglas wanted iron kettle drums and carved wooden drumsticks to accompany any and all forms of peyote rituals. He must have a full sequence of peyote equipment—or whatever else he happened to be collecting at the time.

To go to Jake's with Dr. Douglas was an exhausting experience. Douglas' shrewdness and thrift were pitted against Jake's knowledge and his determination to show some sort of profit, even from a man whom he greatly liked and admired. There were no chairs in the store. Indian women could sit on the floor if they wanted to, but that was hardly a position for one who accompanied a museum director. The bargaining could go on all day.

The only solution was to sit in the car parked at the curb—and miss all the fun. Besides, there was always the possibility that Dr. Douglas would charge into the street with a leonine roar: "Come back in here and tell me what *you* think of this!" It was all-too-public shopping, with Indians also sitting in cars parked along the street, looking on and commenting.

When Jake became terminally ill, Irma took over the shop. She could not give it her full time, because she had to care for her father, and the door was often locked. It was a sad and heavy time for everyone. When Jake died he was given an Indian funeral followed by a Scottish Rite service.

Irma was of the same determined character as her father. She cleaned up the shop, got some new equipment and went into business at the old stand on Broadway. Most structures along the Indian Main Street had not been face-lifted, and Irma carefully left the exterior of the building as it was. She put her father's old Packard sedan up on blocks in the garage, partly out of sentiment because "Papa always drove Packards," and partly from business acumen, because "Someday somebody's going to want to collect the last model Packard made."

The only time we ever saw two thousand dollars in crisp new tens and twenties was the time Irma was tried in federal court. This was in Oklahoma City.

After keeping a migratory bird treaty with Canada on the books for years without doing anything about it, the United States Congress listened to the pleas of the Audubon Society and decided to save our predatory birds.

Now, as it happens, peyote fans are *supposed* to be made from the feathers of predators. Eagle, hawk, flycatcher and road-runner feathers are particularly desirable. Flycatchers are not predators, but their swift, darting flight gives an appearance of great strength and power. Best of all are the crimped wing feathers of water turkeys or North American cormorants, and they are predators.

Jake had stocked peyote fans for years, supplying Dr. Douglas, the Indians and anyone else who wanted to buy fans. There was an abundant supply of predatory bird feathers on hand in his shop when the government decided to enforce the treaty.

One method of enforcement was to purchase feathers from known dealers, on one excuse or another, and then to bring an indictment against the sellers. If the game warden who made the purchase was a white man feathers disappeared from showcases before he could enter a store.

Irma's case was different from others. She knew the law was being enforced, and she thought she knew all the Indians in western Oklahoma. One day a man, unmistakably Indian, a Navaho, appeared in her store with a pitiful tale to tell. His father, out at Fort Defiance, Arizona, was dying. Only a peyote curing ceremony could save him, and they had no fan to use in the ritual. Would Irma—could Irma—? And although she knew the maximum fine for such an offense was two thousand dollars, Irma could and did.

The Navaho was a game warden.

We wrote to Irma and offered to testify that the fans the warden had impounded were very old; that some of them must have been in the shop for as long as fifty years. We added that we could prove it (as expert witnesses, modestly) by the designs on the handles and the beads used to execute them. Irma accepted, as much because she wanted feminine company as because she wanted expert testimony, we suspect.

The day came, a scorcher in July. Irma appeared in the air-conditioned courtroom newly clad, inside and out, from head to toe. Her sisters had provided a whole, new, very becoming outfit. And Irma brought her own expert witnesses; peyote priests who could swear to the fact that other feathers would be inacceptable for ceremonial fans. Her attorney accompanied them.

Finally, the case came to revolve around a fan made of road-runner feathers. Was the road runner—the *paisano* of Texas and New Mexico—a predator or not? The game wardens contended that it was, because it broke into quail nests and ate the eggs, even if it did not attack adult quail. The court admitted that he, himself, indulged occasionally in quail hunting. Eventually he decided that rather than have his fun spoiled he would declare the road runner a predatory bird. He leveled the minimum fine of one hundred twenty dollars.

"Come to the ladies' room with me," Irma whispered. It seemed a reasonable request. We had all been sitting in the courtroom for three hours. We could feel certain biological stirrings ourselves.

Instead of retiring to a screened cubicle, however, Irma

stood before us, arms outstretched. "Please help me roll this girdle down," she requested. "It's so new it's stiff."

We obliged. Packed against Irma's waist, tight inside the girdle, were the two thousand dollars in ten- and twenty-dollar bills. Irma counted out the one hundred twenty dollars she needed, and we shook her back into the girdle. "Aren't they hot?" we asked, awed.

"Pretty hot," Irma replied, "and you'd never believe how scratchy they are!"

Whether it was the preposterous Max Meyer of Sapulpa, as his writing son calls him; Rabbi Joseph Blatt of Oklahoma City, who served with all his scholarship, wisdom and kindness the first Reformed Jewish congregation in the city; the emigrant from Hungary who sold wagonloads of ice and barrels full of water to the men and women who waited at the Kansas line for the opening of the Cherokee strip, and then took up the nearest townsite and went into business selling ice in summer and coal in winter; the college friend who, when her date asked her to repeat her name, snapped, "My name's Becky Finkelstein and my daddy's a junk dealer. Do you want to make something out of it?" (he was the biggest dealer in second-hand oil field equipment in the state), the Jews of Oklahoma are an honored and a loved part of their communities. They staked their claims, and they held them.

Nathan Court, professor of mathematics at the University of Oklahoma, persuaded an old school friend, Albert Einstein, to leave Hitler's Germany for the United States. Dr. Ernest Lachmann, who joined the faculty of the University of Oklahoma as professor of anatomy, came to the state at about the same time Dr. Einstein went to Princeton. Dr. Lachmann and his students have enlarged the reputation of the Medical

School greatly. Dr. Court was said to be the only man besides Dr. Einstein to completely understand the theory of relativity. Such men cannot be omitted from this book. They, as much as anyone else, are a part of Oklahoma. They have staked their claims and they have held them. Until the 1930s few Oklahomans had ever heard of anti-Semitism.

CHAPTER 22

WHAT DO YOU DO TO GET A DOCTOR?

Mention of Dr. Lachmann and of Fort Everett in previous chapters brings up the question of medicine and medical research, fields in which Oklahomans are particularly proud of their resources. Whatever joking we may have done about the construction of Fort Everett, the fact remains that Mark Allen Everett, M.D., professor of dermatology at the University of Oklahoma Medical School, is a man of international stature and recognition, an art collector and a balletomane who has made possible many valuable experiences for his community. If he likes poured concrete construction on land he has given to the Medical School he is certainly entitled to have it, and we probably should apologize for our flippancy.

Dr. Everett is also the only medical practitioner we know who sends his patients to an Indian "medicine man" in Seminole. This man specializes in the treatment of certain kinds of warts, and removes them with his own secret method. Name us another doctor of medicine who would have the courage and humility to do the same thing.

The Medical School had its beginnings on the University of Oklahoma campus in Norman. It was housed in a frame building which had barely space for dissection, was inadequately heated and lighted and was quickly outgrown. The university proper had opened its classes in 1890, and the first students enrolled in the Medical School two years later. There was only a two-year preparatory course at first, and when it was completed students went on to other universities to complete their doctoral work.

As soon as possible the course was increased to a full four years, and the Medical School became one of the few in the United States to receive an "A" rating from the American Medical Association.

The frame structure was replaced by a three-story brick building, which included classrooms, laboratories, workrooms and a medical museum. It still could not accommodate all the students who applied for admission, and it lacked clinical facilities. In 1928, the Board of Regents of the university voted to move the Medical School to Oklahoma City, where hospitals were already offering clinical opportunities to students, and the building that was first known as the University Hospital has now become a medical complex which, including the Department of Dermatology, extends for almost a mile along North East Thirteenth Street, with Veterans' Administration facilities at one end of the row and the new Presbyterian Hospital complex at the other.

After the removal of the Medical School to Oklahoma City, the building which formerly had housed it became the School of Pharmacy. Behind it stretched a belt of meadowland and trees, where cadavers had been disposed of after their removal from the dissecting rooms. This fact was forgotten in time, and as the university campus grew, a new south oval, beyond the original campus, was begun.

There was great need for a building to house the social sciences, and excavations started directly south of the Pharmacy Building. Then one day a great hue and cry went up. All anthropologists front and center! Bones had been found in the red clay soil south of the Pharmacy Building. Perhaps it was a hitherto unknown and unsuspected Indian burial ground.

Of course it happened at lunchtime. When one of us returned from having lunch with a publisher to resume work at the university's Stovall Museum, it was to find herself bereft of colleagues. Not only anthropologists but paleontologists were down on their knees in the red mud, toiling with trowels and brushes to clean the bones as they excavated the remains. The one member of the museum staff who had actually been a student at the university when the building was in use as a Medical School and the land to the south became an informal cemetery laughed so hard that she literally could not explain to the other staff members what the joke was.

It would not be fair to end a discussion of the Medical School without mentioning Mark R. Everett, Ph.D., usually referred to as "Dr. Everett, Sr."

A Harvard graduate, a native of Pennsylvania and a man as dedicated as his son, Dr. Everett retired after thirty years as professor of biology and dean of the Medical School to become dean emeritus and to write the history of the medical profession in Oklahoma.

But still, with graduating classes now running into the hundreds, what do you do to get a doctor? There has been a natural tendency for doctors to cluster in the major cities of the state, where opportunities for clinical experience and private practice are greatest. This leaves many of the smaller towns in Oklahoma without physicians. The University of Tulsa, in another intensely concentrated population area, is already making plans for opening a second medical school of its own. The problem of small-town medical practices is not as acute in Oklahoma as in Texas and New Mexico, for instance, where there are whole counties without physicians, although Texas is well provided with medical schools of high caliber. New Mexico, as yet, does not have a medical school.

Nor can we fail to mention Allen Stanley, Ph.D., professor emeritus of physiology, geneticist of international reputation, and locally known as "the rat man." Dr. Stanley has developed a strain of sterile but vigorous male rats, which go through the motions of mating with wild females but produce no offspring. It is Dr. Stanley's great hope to see the day when his fighting male rats will clear out the other males who are capable of reproduction, and rats will be no more.

It is our own hope to see every town in Oklahoma, regardless of size, supplied with physicians and with clinical and hospital facilities. That time is still to come, but it is not the fault of the men who have built and are building the Medical School of the University of Oklahoma.

CHAPTER 23

CADILLACS FOR MEXICO

Of all the so-called minority groups who have done most to "advance their image," the most striking are those of Mexican birth and their descendants. But in the beginning was the word, and the word was "greaser." "Spic" was heard sometimes, and "dirty Mexicans" often, but by and large those of Mexican birth or descent were greasers. They, like the Chinese, had come into Oklahoma with railroads, and they clung to the rails as to life lines, huddling in shanty towns, doing menial labor, clinging to each other, their own language, and what shreds of their culture they had been able to preserve. Only their church helped and protected them for many years.

The word greaser derived from the supposed fact that Mexican food—even in Mexico—is characterized by great amounts of floating fat. Anyone who has ever been to Mexico knows that the food there is varied and delicious—and not greasy. It was a far step above the fat-back, four-hour-boiled "greens" and corn pone and molasses of many other Oklahoma settlers. Other people were not invited into Spanish-American homes to judge for themselves, as a rule.

One man changed all that. He gave the Spanish-American community dignity and the respect of other Oklahomans. Luis Alvarado came north to Oklahoma from Monterrey, Mexico, in about 1930. He was red-headed and fair-skinned, like many descendants of the people of northern Spain. He spoke little English, but he knew what he wanted—a restaurant that wasn't greasy. And so, on the north side of Twenty-third Street, west of the capitol, in a middle-class, respectable area of small businessmen, far from the shanty towns of the railroads, he opened one. He was his own cook; often his own dishwasher, bus boy and waiter.

The food was clean, tasty, inexpensive and not greasy. Other members of the family came to take over some of Luis' multiple duties, and the restaurant prospered; prospered so much it had to move to larger quarters, near St. Anthony Hospital, which was the one preferred by Mexican-Americans when they or members of their families were ill. The new and larger restaurant was discovered by doctors, nurses and technicians, and the word spread through the Anglo-American community that this was *the* place to eat, if you wanted something different, served in pleasant surroundings.

Again Mr. Alvarado outgrew his space. Few people stopped to think that the name Alvarado was an ancient and honorable one in Spain and Mexico. They were aware of unfailing courtesy and graciousness, as their host turned over kitchen duties to younger members of the family, and became his own maitre d'hotel.

This time Mr. Alvarado *built* his own restaurant. G. A. Nichols, a real estate developer, had taken a small diagonal street in the northwest part of town; had its name changed from 30th Place to El Paseo, and constructed a faintly Mediterranean-Spanish Village. (He filled in the best crawdad fishing hole in metropolitan Oklahoma City to do it, but that's pure nostalgia.) What better place than a Spanish village for a Mexican restaurant? The new El Charrito was built, and much time and money went into planning and decorating it.

And again there was too much business for the location. By this time most of the Alvarados in Monterrey seemed to have moved to Oklahoma City. It was still a family operation, but one man could not be in two places at once. A chain of El Charrito restaurants, each under the direction of a brother or a *primo*, spread over Oklahoma City, and reached out to Tulsa and to Wichita, Kansas, and on to Atlanta, Georgia. New dishes were added to the once-simple menu.

Eventually, El Charrito merged with the El Chico food products and restaurant chain of Texas. After all, the owners of that firm were *primos*, too. The announcement of the merger was a newspaper advertisement, illustrated with a photograph of all concerned standing with joined hands under the caption "One El of a Family."

While all this was going on, other things were changing, too. The Roman Catholic Church of the Little Flower—"the Mexican church"—began following the examples of other churches by holding bazaars and bingo games. Mexico's two Independence Days, the Fifth of May and the Sixteenth of September, were celebrated with formal balls, open to all the public and, of course, featuring the great Anglo-American institution, the princess of the ball, in the ballroom of the Civic Center. Spanish began to be taught in high schools as a useful second language for business majors. A Mexican consulate was established to handle international affairs.

To convince everybody that Oklahoma City really was friendly to its neighbors from south of the border, Mr. Alvarado executed a stroke of genius. He organized a caravan. A long line of super Cadillacs drove south to Monterrey from Oklahoma City, and many and joyous were the reunions when the Cadillacs to Mexico arrived there. The Cadillacs had gone to Monterrey half-empty, but they came back loaded to the roofs. It was the finest piece of advertising anyone could have devised—for both countries.

Mr. Alvarado, our hair has gone from red to gray in the years since one of us ate her first enchiladas and sopapillas in the little place on Twenty-third Street, but your courtesy is as charming as ever, your restaurant as clean, and your menu is still expanding, if your waistline isn't. You gave at least one Oklahoman the incentive to visit your city and the country where you were born, to learn its language, and to try to master its complicated cuisine. *Muchisimas gracias, Senor.* Thank you. *¡Y Ole!*

CHAPTER 24

TO WIND IT ALL UP

How does one thank the people who have contributed to a book that comprises most of one life and a third of another? Memories stretch, but not far enough. Some names must of necessity be omitted by default.

First, perhaps, is the late Sydney Kenner Cunningham Marriott, a prolific writer and devoted reader of letters, who probably never voluntarily threw away a piece of paper in her life. She worked as secretary, and later as accountant (she was a CPA) for the long-defunct Sammies Oil Company, in the early wildcatting days, and her records of early oil men have been of immeasurable help.

Dorothy Forsyth Anderson, of Oklahoma City, contributed some anecdotes of her father's struggles to construct a domeless capitol, and supported and confirmed other memories.

The indefatigable Rella Looney, of the Oklahoma Historical Society, is in a class by herself when it comes to contributions to research. Nobody can do any research on Oklahoma without eventually appealing to Mrs. Looney.

The president of the Oklahoma Historical Society and former mayor of Oklahoma City, George Shirk, seemed never to be too busy to assist with out-of-the-way bits of information.

Many of those we have mentioned by name during the writing of the text are still very much alive and kicking, and this can be taken as a blanket acknowledgment of their kindness, generous memories and the "living history" that flows day by day, instead of settling into stagnant pools divided by dates.

The city of Muskogee is in a class by itself and must be experienced to be believed. We owe thanks there, too, for the convincing experience of opening a museum with a board of directors who thought the director of a museum was just another member of the board.

To our colleagues at Central State University, Garland Godfrey, Ph.D., president; Joe C. Jackson, Ph.D., vice-president in charge of academic affairs; Alvin Alcorn, vice-president in charge of financial affairs; Frank Finney, Jr., Ph.D., Dean of the School of Liberal Arts; Cliff Warren, Ph.D., professor of creative arts—to all these and many more of the university's personnel, we owe our humble and hearty thanks.

Our gratitude is due also to Wayne Bowman, of Seminoff, Bowman and Bode, architects, Oklahoma City, for indispensable factual information.

E. G. "Ty" Dahlgren of Oklahoma City and Rudolph and Susan Brauchli of Muri, Berne, Switzerland, gave us many sidelights on the early years of oil development in Oklahoma.

Without Dr. Mark R. Everett, who is writing his own

history of the University of Oklahoma's Medical School, we would have floundered, as he has, through a maze of reports.

And to Pat Reeves, of Central State University, we are indebted for much assistance with the preparation of this manuscript.

To our students, who furnished us with many otherwise unobtainable bits of information, and to our student assistant, Lawanna Kent Brown, who helped with typing and research, we can only say that we owe them a debt only time can repay.

Carol Rachlin says that Indians brought her to Oklahoma and it is a good thing they did, for she was able with their help to record many often overlooked bits of information. Her special thanks go to Ed and Mary Mack and Bea Patterson, of Shawnee, Lucy Griggs of Oklahoma City, George and Betty Dowd of Del City, the late Isadore and Mary Neal of Cushing, the late Sadie Feder, of Shawnee; all of them Sauk and Fox. They taught her as an Indian mother teaches a child, "Just keep on a-goin'" and there could have been no better advice.

We have kept on a-goin' even when the goin' got rough, because good Oklahomans, wherever they were born, do just that. We staked our claims in this our Oklahoma, and come hell or high water we've held them.

OKLAHOMA—THE THIRD STATE SONG?

O—is for oil because we have lots of it here,
K—is for the kind, happy and cheerful folks you'll find everywhere,
L—is for love and here it grows and grows,
A—is for always, because this state is always on its toes.
H—is for happiness because of our lack of fears,
O—is for only, only the best meat, that is, because you see, we raise a lot of steers,
M—is for the many lakes we have. I hope you brought some bait,
    And
A—again stands for always, because you are always welcome to our state.

Text by Mishael McMillian
1008 Locust Lane,
Midwest City, Oklahoma.
With permission of the author.
(Aged ten when she wrote it in 1970)

BIBLIOGRAPHY

Alford, Thomas Wilcat (as told to Florence Drake), *Civilization*. Norman, Oklahoma, University of Oklahoma Press, 1936.

Allen, James B., *The Company Town in the American West*. Norman, Oklahoma, University of Oklahoma Press, 1966.

Anderson, Edgar, *Plants, Man and Life*. Boston, Massachusetts, Little, Brown and Company, 1952.

Aydelotte, Dora, *Green Gravel*. New York, New York, D. Appleton-Century Company, 1937.

Bass, Althea, *Cherokee Messenger*. Norman, Oklahoma, University of Oklahoma Press, 1936.

Battey, Thomas C., *The Life and Adventures of a Quaker Among the Indians*. (Introduction by Alice Marriott.) Norman, Oklahoma, University of Oklahoma Press, 1968.

Bourke, John G., *On the Border with Crook*. New York, New York, Charles Scribner's Sons, 1891. Reprinted, Columbus, Ohio. Long's College Book Company, 1950.

Bryant, Keith L., Jr., *Alfalfa Bill Murray*. Norman, Oklahoma, University of Oklahoma Press, 1968.

Custer, Elizabeth B., *"Boots and Saddles" or Life in Dakota with General Custer*. (Introduction by Jane R. Stewart.) Norman, Oklahoma, University of Oklahoma Press, 1961.

Dale, Edward Everett, *Oklahoma. The Story of a State*. Evanston, Illinois, Row, Peterson and Company, 1949.

Debo, Angie, *Oklahoma*. Norman, Oklahoma, University of Oklahoma Press, 1949.

Everett, Mark Reuben, *Pioneering for Medical Research*. Oklahoma City, Oklahoma, University of Oklahoma Medical Center, 1966.

——, *Medical Education in Oklahoma*. Norman, Oklahoma, University of Oklahoma Press, 1972.

Foreman, Grant, *Sequoyah*. Norman, Oklahoma, University of Oklahoma Press, 1938.

——, *A History of Oklahoma*. Norman, Oklahoma, University of Oklahoma Press, 1942.

Gibson, A. M., *The Kickapoos. Lords of the Middle Border*. Norman, Oklahoma, University of Oklahoma Press, 1963.

Gittinger, Roy, *The Formation of the State of Oklahoma (1803–1906)*. Norman, Oklahoma, University of Oklahoma Press, 1939.

Golden, Harry, *Forgotten Pioneer*. New York, New York, a Fawcett Crest Book, 1966.

Graham, R. B. Cunninghame, *The Horses of the Conquest*. Norman, Oklahoma, University of Oklahoma Press, 1949.

Gregg, Elinor D., *The Indians and the Nurse*. Norman, Oklahoma, University of Oklahoma Press, 1965.

Gregory, Jack, *Sam Houston with the Cherokees (1829–1833)*. Austin, Texas, University of Texas Press, 1967.

Hagan, William T., *The Sac and Fox Indian*. Norman, Oklahoma, University of Oklahoma Press, 1958.

Harris, Foster, *The Look of the Old West*. New York, New York, The Viking Press, 1955.

BIBLIOGRAPHY

Hines, Gordon, *Alfalfa Bill*. Oklahoma City, Oklahoma, Oklahoma Press, 1932.

Hoebel, Adamson E. and Wallace, Ernest, *The Comanches*. Norman, Oklahoma, University of Oklahoma Press, 1952.

Hofstadter, Richard, Aaron, Daniel and Miller, William, *The American Republic*. Volume I—Discovery to 1865, Volume II—Since 1866. Englewood Cliffs, New Jersey, Prentice-Hall, 1959.

Hoig, Stan, *The Sand Creek Massacre*. Norman, Oklahoma, University of Oklahoma Press, 1961.

Hollon, W. Eugene, *Beyond the Cross Timbers*. Norman, Oklahoma, University of Oklahoma Press, 1955.

Howard, Robert West, *This Is the West*. Chicago, Illinois, Rand McNally and Company, 1957.

Hyams, Edward, *Soil and Civilization*. London, England, Thames and Hudson, 1952.

Kappler, Charles J. (compiled and edited), *Laws and Treaties*. Volume II—Treaties. Washington, D.C., Government Printing Office, 1904.

Kilpatrick, Jack Frederick and Gritts, Anna, *Walk in Your Soul*. Dallas, Texas, Southern Methodist University Press, 1965.

——— (translated and edited), *The Shadow of Sequoyah*. Social Documents of the Cherokees 1862–1964. Norman, Oklahoma, University of Oklahoma Press, 1965.

Knight, Oliver, *Following the Indian Wars*. Norman, Oklahoma, University of Oklahoma Press, 1960.

La Barre, Weston, *The Peyote Cult*. New Haven, Connecticut, Yale University Press, 1938.

Lawton Business and Professional Woman's Club (initiated and assembled), *'Neath August Sun, 1901*. Anadarko, Oklahoma, N. T. Plummer Printing Co., 1929.

Lee, Nelson, *Three Years Among the Comanches*. (Introduction by Walter Prescott Webb.) Norman, Oklahoma, University of Oklahoma Press, 1957.

Lowie, Robert H., *Indians of the Plains*. Anthropological Handbook Number I. Published for the American Museum of Natural History. New York, New York, McGraw-Hill Book Company, Inc., 1954.

Marcy, Randolph, *Adventure on Red River* (edited and annotated by Grant Foreman). Norman, Oklahoma, University of Oklahoma Press, 1937.

Marriott, Alice, *The Ten Grandmothers*. Norman, Oklahoma, University of Oklahoma Press, 1954.

Marriott, Alice and Rachlin, Carol K., *Peyote*. New York, New York, Thomas Y. Crowell Company, 1971.

Marriott, Alice, Faulconer, Estelle and McReynolds, Edwin G., *Oklahoma. The Story of Its Past and Present*. Norman, Oklahoma, University of Oklahoma Press, 1961; revised edition, 1967.

Mathews, John Joseph, *Wah'Kon-Tah*. Norman, Oklahoma, University of Oklahoma Press, 1932.

———, *Talking to the Moon*. Chicago, Illinois, University of Chicago Press, 1945.

———, *Life and Death of an Oil Man*. Norman, Oklahoma, University of Oklahoma Press, 1951.

———, *The Osages, Children of Middle Waters*. Norman, Oklahoma, University of Oklahoma Press, 1961.

Mayhall, Mildred P., *The Kiowas*. Norman, Oklahoma, University of Oklahoma Press, 1962.

McCullum, Henry D. and Frances T., *The Wire That Fenced the West*. Norman, Oklahoma, University of Oklahoma Press, 1965.

Meyer, Lewis, *Preposterous Papa.* Cleveland, Ohio, World Publishing Company, 1959.

———, *Mostly Mama.* Garden City, New York, Doubleday & Company, 1971.

Miller, Floyd, *Bill Tilghman.* Garden City, New York, Doubleday & Company, 1968.

Milsten, David Randolph, *Thomas Gilcrease.* Norman, Oklahoma, The Naylor Company, 1969.

Nye, Wilbur Sturtevant, *Carbine and Lance.* Norman, Oklahoma, University of Oklahoma Press, 1942.

———, *Bad Medicine & Good.* Norman, Oklahoma, University of Oklahoma Press, 1962.

Oklahoma Historical Society, *Chronicles of Oklahoma.* Volume X, Number IV. Oklahoma City, Oklahoma, 1932.

———, *The Chronicles of Oklahoma.* Volume XLII, Number 3, Fall. Oklahoma City, Oklahoma, 1964.

Prettyman, W. S. *Indian Territory* (selected and edited by Robert E. Cunningham). Norman, Oklahoma, University of Oklahoma Press, 1957.

Rister, Carl Coke, *Land Hunger.* Norman, Oklahoma, University of Oklahoma Press, 1942.

Ruth, Kent, *How to Enjoy Your Western Vacations.* Norman, Oklahoma, University of Oklahoma Press, 1956.

———, *Oklahoma.* A Guide to the Sooner State. Norman, Oklahoma, University of Oklahoma Press, 1957.

———, *Great Day in the West.* Norman, Oklahoma, University of Oklahoma Press, 1963.

Sandoz, Mari, *Cheyenne Autumn.* New York, New York, McGraw-Hill Book Company, 1953.

———, *The Buffalo Hunters.* The Story of the Hide Men. New York, New York, Hasting House, 1954.

Saunderson, Mont H., *Western Land and Water Use*. Norman, Oklahoma, University of Oklahoma Press, 1950.

Schmitt, Martin F., *General George Crook*. Norman, Oklahoma, University of Oklahoma Press, 1946.

Seger, John H., *Early Days Among the Cheyenne and Arapaho Indians*. Norman, Oklahoma, University of Oklahoma Press, 1956.

Shepperson, Wilbur S., *Emigration and Disenchantment*. Norman, Oklahoma, University of Oklahoma Press, 1965.

White, E. E., *Experiences of A Special Indian Agent*. Norman, Oklahoma, University of Oklahoma Press, 1965.

Wissler, Clark, *The American Indian*, New York, New York, Douglas C. McMurtrie, 1917.

INDEX

Aeronautics, School of, 145–146
Afton, Okla., 8
Ahyoka, 153, 154, 155
Alcoholic beverages, 75–76, 139–41, 178
Alcorn, Alvin, 220
Alva, Okla., 37, 57
Alvarado, Luis, 216ff.
American Institute of Architecture, 116
Amish, 131
Anadarko, Okla., 201–7
Anderson, Dorothy Forsyth, 219
Anglicans, 113
Animal life (fauna), xii, xiii. *See also* specific animals
Apache, Okla., 49–50
Apache Indians, 10, 41, 49
Appaloosa horses, 32
Arapaho, Okla., 63
Arapaho Indians, 10, 38, 41, 45, 131; Darlington Agency and, 193ff.; land opened, 63ff.
Arbuckle Mountains, 4
Archaeology, 186
Architecture, xv–xvi, 109–11, 115–16 (*see also* Building and construction; specific buildings); state capitol, 82–84
Arkansas River, 7, 17, 44, 135
Armadillos, xiii
Army Corps of Engineers, 189
Automobiles, 68. *See also* Roads
Aydelotte, Dora, 144

Bailey, H. E., Turnpike, 42
Baker, Bryant, 96
Baltimore Belle, the, 113–14
Barrow, Clyde, 146
Bartlesville, Okla., 87, 97, 99, 109
Bartlett, Dewey, 44
Basques, xix
Battey, Thomas C. (Thomissey), 50–52
Baum Building, 116
Baxter Springs, Kans., 40
Bayo coyote horses, 33
Beauty, 142–43
Beaver River, 191
Big Cabin Creek, 47–48
Big Pasture, 65
Big Tree (chief), 50
Biloxi Indians, 21
Black Kettle, 49
Blatt, Joseph, 208
Blue Eagle, 102, 103
Bluestem, 5
Boats, 42, 43, 192
Boley, Okla., 131
Books and writers, 144
Boomers, 9, 58–62
Bootlegging, 140, 141
Boudinot, Elias, 171
Boudinot family, 19
Bowman, Wayne, 220
Brandt, Joseph, 144
Brauchli, Rudolph, 88, 89, 220
Brauchli, Susan, 88, 89, 220
Bricks, 66–67
Bristow, Okla., 66
Broken Bow, Okla., 129–30
Brown, Lawanna Kent, 221
Buffalo, 39

INDEX

Building and construction, 66–67, 105–11, 194. *See also* architecture
Bull-dogging steers, 120
Bureau of Indian Affairs, 23, 160, 174, 175, 199

Caddo Indians, 50
California, 37–38
Calumet, Okla., 63
Campbell, Walter Stanley, 198
Canadian River, 81–82, 190–91
Cannon, "Uncle Joe," 178
Canton (Cantonment), 48, 191
Capitol building, 81–85; portraits in, 85 (*see also* specific persons)
Carlisle Indian School, 161
Catoosa, Port of, 44
Cattle, 8, 35, 40–41, 94, 192. *See also* Rodeos
Central State University, 108, 220
Chandler, Okla., 66
Charleston (dance), 144
Charrito, El, 217
Cherokee Indians, 16–20, 21, 43, 52, 56–57, 170–71. *See also* Rogers, Will; Sequoyah
Cherokee National Press, 21–22, 170–71
Cherokee Phoenix, The, 22
Cheyenne, Okla., 68
Cheyenne Indians, 10, 38, 41, 45, 52, 193–94, 195; Labor Day powwow at Colony, 200; land opened, 63ff.
Chickasaw Indians, 16, 20, 21, 24, 37, 42, 43, 74, 127, 128; and Constitutional Convention, 76; as saddle makers, 35
Chico, El, 217
Chinese, 123–25
Chisholm Trail, 40–41
Choctaw Indians, 16, 19ff., 36, 42, 43, 73, 127, 128, 186
Choctaw Mining Company, 127
Choctaw Oil and Refining Company, 87
Chouteau, Pierre, 7
Cimarron River, 79
Circuses, 119
Citizen's Bank Tower, 109
Citizen's National Bank, 109
Civilian Conservation Corps (CCC), 185–86

Civil War, 43, 46–49
Claims, staking. *See* Homesteading
Claremore, Okla., 157, 160
Clay beds, 66
Cleveland, Grover, 60, 71
Climate, 192
Clinton, Okla., 63
Clothes, 113, 141–42, 143
Coal, xii, 127–28
Coffeyville, Kans., 66
Colcord, Charles, 116–17
Colleges. *See* Schools and education; specific colleges
Colony, Okla., 130, 196–200
Columbus, Diego, 103
Comanche Indians, 10, 25, 38, 41, 49, 50; language, 156
Connecticut Yankee at the Court of King Arthur, A (film), 159
Conner and Pojezny, 109
Constitution, 75ff., 143
Construction. *See* Building and construction
Coolidge, Calvin, 140, 159
Corn, Okla., 130
Coronado, Francisco de, 5
Cotton, 94–95
Couch, Glenn, 60
Court, Nathan, 208–9
Crawford, Joan, 144
Creek Indians, 16, 19ff., 23–24, 43, 153; Alice Robertson and orphans, 174
Criterion Theatre (Oklahoma City), 119
Cross, Minnie Bear, 196–97, 199
Cross, Robert, 196, 197, 199
Cross Timbers, 3, 5–6, 8–9, 37, 38, 56ff.
Croy, Homer, 159
Cunningham, Max, 27–28, 41, 81ff., 135ff., 185; and bootlegging, 141
Cunningham, Philip, 135ff.
Cunningham, Sydney. *See* Marriott, Sydney Kenner Cunningham
Curtis, Charles, 144
Custer, George, 49
Czechs, xviii, 130

Dahlgren, E. G. "Ty," 88–89, 220
Dale, Edward Everett, 106
Dams, 189–92
Dancers, 144

INDEX

Dappled gray horses, 33
Darlington, Brinton, 193, 194
Darlington, Okla., xvii, 52, 193-95
David Harum (film), 159
Davidson, Jo, 160
Davis, Okla., 45
Dawes, Henry, 181
Dawes Commission, 71, 72, 181
Deer family, 23
De Golyer Collection, 106
Delaware, Okla., 8
Delaware Indians, 52; language, 156
Delmar Gardens, 116, 117
Democratic Party, 76
De Soto, Hernando, 5
Dodge City, Kans., 40, 46
Dogs, 28-30, 31
Douglas, Frederic, 204-5
Dowd, George and Betty, 221
Dull Knife, 52
Dutch Reformed Church, 196, 197

Eakins, Thomas, 103
Early Days Among the Cheyenne and Arapaho Indians, 198-99
East Shawnee Trail, 40
Edmond. *See* Central State University
Edmondson, J. Howard, 85, 163
Education. *See* Schools and education
Edward VII, 120, 121
Edwards house, 116
Einstein, Albert, 208-9
Elmira College, 173
El Reno, Okla., 48
Enid, Okla., 87
Episcopalians, 113-114, 196
Erick, Okla., 63
Erosion checks, 189
Ether and Me (Rogers), 158
Everett, Mark Allen, 110, 211
Everett, Mark R., 213, 220-21

Fairs, 119
Fans, peyote, 204-5, 206-8
Farm ponds, 189-90
Faucett Ranch, 87
Feder, Sadie, 221
Federal Oil and Gas Commission, 91-92
Ferber, Edna, 201
Field, Clark, 101
Finkelstein, Becky, 208

Finney, Frank, Jr., 220
First Christian Church (Oklahoma City), 109-10
Fishing, 191-92
Five Civilized Tribes, 16-25, 43, 67, 71ff. (*see also* specific tribes); and law enforcement, 55-56; Light Horsemen, 34, 47; and slaves, 46-47, 48
Five Civilized Tribes Museum, 42-43, 179
Flowers. *See* Plant life
Floyd, Pretty Boy, 146
Foreign-language settlements, xvii-xix. *See also* specific groups
Foreman, Carolyn Thomas, 182, 184, 187
Foreman, Grant, 181-87
Forsyth, George, xvi, 82, 83, 110
Fort Arbuckle, 45
Fort Gibson, 7, 17, 34, 37, 42
Fort Reno, xvii, 46, 48, 59-60, 193
Fort Sill, xvii, 48, 59, 60
Fort Smith, 37
Fort Supply, 45-46, 48, 191
Franz, Fritz, 76
Freedmen, 131-32
Fuller, Buckminster, 109
Fullerton, Eula, 185

Geary, Okla., 130
Georgia, 18
Germans, xvii-xviii, 130-31
Geronimo, 49-50
Ghost Dance, 63
Gilcrease, Thomas, 91, 95, 101-3
Gilcrease Institute, 101-3
Gist. *See* Guest
Givvens, Joshua, 196-97
Glenn Pool, 91
Glover River, 4
Goats' milk, 128-29
Godfrey, Garland, 220
Golden, Harry, 201
Grandfather clause, 77
Grand River, 7, 190
Grand River Dam Authority, 190
Grant, Ulysses S., 193
Grapes of Wrath, The, 184-85
Graveure, Louis, 118
"Greaser," 215
"Great Raft," 6-7, 42
Great Western Trail, 40-41

Great White House, The, 120–21
Green Grow the Lilacs, 15
Griggs, Lucy, 221
Grullo horses, 33
Guest, George, 152
Guest, George. See Sequoyah
Guest, Nathaniel, 151, 152
Gustavus, King, 161
Guthrie, Okla., 67, 76, 79–81
Guymon, Okla., 8

Hales, William, house, 115–16
Hall, David, 44
Hall of Fame, 167; Cowboy, 120, 122
Hammerstein, Oscar, II, 15
Harding, Warren G., 139–40
Hartshorne, Okla., 129
Haskell, Charles, 80
Hassrick, Royal, 204
Haubiel, Felice, 144
Hayes, Helen, 118
Heffner, Lake, 191
Heffner, Roy, 116
Highway 9, 42
Historical Society, 84, 145, 171, 183–84, 187, 199
Hitchiti Indians, 21
Homesteading (land openings), 9–12, 57–62, 63–66, 77–78
Hopkins-Dukes, Amos, 10
Horses, 30, 31–36. See also Rodeos
Houses, 115–16 (See also specific homes); mansions of the oil-rich (see Oil; specific homes, museums); sod, xvi
Houston, Sam, 17, 153
Huckins Hotel, 81, 83
Hugo, Okla., 119
Hurt, Victor, 100

Illinois River, 7
Indian City, U.S.A., 204
Indians, 7, 10, 13–25, 45–53, 55–57, 63ff., 151–64 (see also Five Civilized Tribes; specific individuals, tribes); and art competition, 101; and beginnings of statehood, 71ff.; and buffalo, 39; Johnny Schmoker's Colony, 193–200; Robertson family and, 170ff.; and travel, 28–36ff.; and voting, 143–44
Indian Territory, 19–25, 45–46, 55–56, 66ff., 170ff. (see also Five Civilized Tribes; Indians; specific places, subjects, tribes); and State of Sequoyah, 75–76
Inkanish, James, 196–97, 199
Inkanish, Mary Little Bear, 196–97, 199–200
Interior, Department of the, 204
Interstate 40, 42
Irving, Washington, 7–8
Italians, xviii, 127–28, 132–33

Jackson, Andrew, 17–18
Jackson, Joe C., 220
James, Overton, 24
Jazz, 145
Jews, 201–9
Johansen, John M., 110
Johnson family, 24
Johnston, Douglas H., 74
Jones, Mr. and Mrs. Fred, 15
Jones, Rupel, Theatre, 109

Keeler, W. W., 24
Kelly, George "Machine Gun" and Kathryn, 146–47
Kendall, Henry, College, 175
Kerr, Grayce Breene, 163
Kerr, Robert Samuel, 43–44, 85, 162–64
Kicking Bird, 50, 52
Kincaide, Reese, 197–98, 199
Kingman, Eugene, 99–100
Kiowa Indians, 10, 25, 38, 41, 49–51, 196–97; language, 156; and saddle making, 34
Kitchen equipment, 22–23
Krebs, Okla., 129
Kress, S. H., Collection, 100–1
Ku Klux Klan, 137–38

Lachman, Ernest, 208–9
Land. See Homesteading; Soils
Langston University, 78, 108
Larrett, Mr. and Mrs. W. R., 146–47
La Salle, Robert Cavelier, sieur de, 17
Laws, 55–56
Lawton, Okla., 48, 118
Layton, Hicks, and Forsyth, 82–83
Lee-Huckins Hotel. See Huckins Hotel

INDEX 235

Light Horsemen, 34, 47
Lindbergh, Charles, 145
Locoweed, 59
Looney, Eula, 185
Looney, Rella, 182, 183, 219-20

McAlester (trader), 127
McAlester, Okla., 118, 127, 129
MacArthur, Douglas, 139
McFadden, Sally, 157
McIntosh family, 20, 23
Mack, Ed and Mary, 221
Marcy, Randolph, 37-38, 57
Marland, Ernest W., 93, 95-97
Marriott, Alice, 201
Marriott, Richard ("Ricardo Marriotti"), 132
Marriott, Sydney Kenner Cunningham, 67-68, 219
Mathews, John Joseph, 118, 144
Medicine, 211-14
Mennonites, 130-31
Mexicans, 215-18
Meyer, Lewis, 201
Meyer, Max, 208
Miami, Okla., 7, 8, 52
Mikasuki Indians, 21
Miles, John D., 194, 195
Miles, Nelson, 52
Milk, 128-29, 198
Miller, Zack, 121
Miller brothers: ranch, 120-21; show, 119, 120
Minco, Okla., 24
Minerva Place, 174-75
Mobilian Indians, 21
Modoc Indians, 50, 51, 52-53
Mohonk Lodge beadwork, 197-98
Mooney, James, 203
Moonshining, 140
Moore, N. B., 199
Moran, Thomas, 103
Mounds, Okla., 131
Mraz, Anabel, 144
Mulhall family show, 119, 157-58
Mummers' Theatre, 110
Murrray, Johnston, 164, 166
Murray, Mary Alice Hearral, 74
Murray, William Henry "Alfalfa Bill," xiii, 120, 151, 164-67; and statehood, 73-74ff.
Music, 144-45
Muskogee, Okla., 7, 44, 75, 79, 87,
181, 182, 220; and fairs, 119; Five Civilized Tribes Museum, 42-43, 179; and Spanish-American War, 175-76, 177; and theater, 118

Natchez Indians, 21
Natchez-on-the-Deep-Fork, xvii
National American Rodeo Cowboys Association, 121-22
Navy, 107-8
Neal, Isadore and Mary, 221
Neergaard, Mrs. William Bigelow, 187
Negroes, 48-49, 78, 108, 120, 135-38; Freedmen's towns, 131-32; and homesteading, 66, 77-78; slaves, 21, 46-47
New Echota, Ga., 155
New Mexico, 36, 214
Nez Percé Indians, 32
Nichols, G. A., 216-17
Nixon, Richard M., 44
Norman. See Oklahoma, University of

Oil, xii, 3, 5, 13-14, 84, 87-95, 117
"Okie," 184
Oklahoma!, 15-16
Oklahoma, University of (Norman), 105-8, 109; School of Medicine, 110-11, 211-13
Oklahoma City, 62, 67-68, 87, 113-17, 185 (*see also* specific buildings, institutions); airport, 160; architecture, xv-xvi, 109-10, 115-16 (*see also* specific buildings); becomes capital, 80ff.; brick plant 66-67; buried city, 123-25; and fairs, 119; Festival of the Arts, 130; Kellys kidnap Urschel in, 146-48; National Cowboy Hall of Fame, 120, 122; rodeo competition in, 122; and theater, 118, 119; trial of Irma Tingley in, 206, 207-8; water supply, 190, 191
Oklahoma City Art Center, 148
Oklahoma City University, 15, 146
Oklahoma Festival of the Arts, 130
Oklahoma Heritage Corporation, 116
Oklahoma Historical Society. See Historical Society
Oklahoma State University, 111
Oklahoma Territory: capital, 79;

opening of, 56-62, 63-69; and statehood, 76
Oklahombi, Joseph, 139
Okmulgee, Okla., 21, 56
"Old Settlers," 16, 17
Oliver, Jennie Harris, 144
Olympics, 161
Oñate, Juan de, 30
Osage Indians, 8, 17, 24, 56, 57, 117-18
Oto Indians, 8, 24, 56-57
Overholser, Henry, 115, 116
Overholser, Lake, 190-91

Paderewski, Ignace, 118
Palomino horses, 33
Parker, Bonnie, 146
Park Hill, 21, 156
Patterson, Bea, 221
Patterson, "Pat," 97, 98, 99
Pavlova, Anna, 118
Pawhuska, Okla., 117-18
Pawnee Bill show, 119
Pawnee Indians, 56
Payne, David, 9, 57-60
Pea Ridge, 48
Philbrook Museum, 99-101
Phillips, Frank, 95, 97, 98, 99, 100, 101; book collection, 106
Phillips, Lee, 95, 97
Phillips, Waite, 95, 97, 99, 100
Philtower, the, 100
Piankasha Indians, 52
Pianos, 42
Pickens, Bill, 120
Pinto horses, 32
Pioneer Days in the Early Southwest (Foreman), 183
Pitcher, Okla., 7, 8
Plant life (flora), xii, xiii, 5-6, 22, 58-59
Ponca City, Okla., xvii, 95-97
Ponca Indians, 17, 56, 120
Porter, Pleasant, 75
Post, Wiley, 158, 159
Poteau, Okla., 164
Powell, John Wesley, 172-73
Prague, Okla., xviii, 130
Pratt, Richard Henry, 161
Price Tower, 109
Prostitutes, 93

Quakers, 50-52, 193ff.

Quapaw Indians, 17, 24, 56
Quarter horses, 33, 35-36

Rachlin, Carol, 221
Railroads, 38-40, 44, 82, 123
Red Fork, Okla., 135
Red River, 6-7, 47, 166
Reeves, Pat, 221
Religion, 113-14, 196-97
Republican Party, 76
Restaurants, 129-30, 216-17
Ridge family, 19
Riggs, Lynn, 15, 16
Ringling Brothers-Barnum & Bailey Circus, 119
Rivers, 6-7, 42, 43, 190-91. *See also* specific rivers
Roads (highways), 27, 41-42
Roan horses, 33
Roberts, Oral, University, 111
Robertson, Alice Mary, 159-60, 169-80
Robertson, Ann Eliza Worcester, 170ff.
Robertson, William, 171-72, 173, 174
Rodeos, 119-22
Rodgers, Richard, 15
Rogers, Betty Blake, 158, 160
Rogers, Clem V., 157
Rogers, John, 16-17
Rogers, Will (William Penn Adair Rogers), 11, 96, 97, 120, 156-60, 165, 179; portrait in capitol, 85, 156, 160
Rogers family, 19, 20
Roman Catholics, 113, 116, 217
Roosevelt, Franklin D., 166
Roosevelt, Theodore, 120, 121, 176, 177
Roper, Norah, 152
Rose, Ralph, 144-45
Ross, John, 17, 19, 21, 155, 156
Ross, Quatie, 155
Ross family, 20
Rothschild's, 117

Saddles, 33-34, 35
St. Paul's Cathedral, 114
Sallisaw, Okla., 184
Salt, 57
San Fernando, Mexico, 156
Santa Fe, N.M., 36

INDEX 237

Santa Fe Trail, 36–37
Sarczyski, "Gran'ma," 133
Sawicki, Janet and Ruth, 133
Sawokla, 175ff.
Sayre, Okla., 63
Schools and education, 21, 77, 78, 105–9 (see also specific schools); medical, 211–14
Schumann-Heink, Ernestine, 118
Seger, John Homer, 194–96, 197
Sells-Floto Circus, 119
Seminoff, Bowman and Bode, 110, 111
Seminoff, George, 110
Seminole, Okla., 87, 88, 93, 211
Seminole Indians, 16, 19, 21, 43
Seneca Indians, 52
Sequoyah, 85, 151–56
Sequoyah Convention, 74–76
Sequoyah Orphan Training School, 175
Shawnee, Okla., xix
Shawnee Trail, 40
Shirk, George, 125, 220
Shoulders, Jim, 122
Sitting Bear, 50
Slaves, 21, 46–47, 48
Smallwood, Norma Des Cygnes, 102
Smith, C. L., 82, 83, 84
Smithsonian Institution: Bureau of Ethnology, 172–73
Smoking, 143
Society of Friends. See Quakers
Sod house, xvi
Soils, 3ff.
Sooners, 62
Southwestern Art Association, 100
Spanish-Americans, 215–18
Spanish-American War, 175–76, 177
Spencer, Okla., xvii
Spiro Collection, 98, 103
"Squaw," 28
Stanley, Allen J., 94, 214
Statehood, 71–78
Steinbeck, John, 184
Stillwater, Okla., 111
Streetcars, 68
Stroud, Okla., 66
Surrey Singers, 15

Taft, Okla., 131
Tahlequah, Okla., 7, 21, 22, 156, 171, 175

Tallchief, Maria and Marjorie, 118
Taos, N.M., 36
Teehee, Houston B., 144
Texas, 6, 7, 17, 46, 47, 166, 214
Texhoma, Lake, 192
Theater, 118–19
They Had to See Paris, 159
Thoburn, Joseph, 145
Thomas, Robert, 181
Thomas-Foreman Home, 18ff., 187
Thorpe, Jim, 85, 161–62
Thorpe, Jim, Museum, 161
Three Forks, 17, 42, 44, 57
Tingley, Irma, 201, 203, 205–8
Tingley, Jacob B., 201–5, 206
Tishomingo, Okla., 21, 73–74
Tonkawa Indians, 52
Tracy, Lee, 119
Transportation, 68. See also specific means
Trapp, Martin, 138
Trees. See Plant life
Tribal court, 55–56
Trueblood, Joshua, 194, 195
Tsa-lah-ghi, 156
Tsali, Okla., 18–19
Tulsa, Okla., 80, 87, 109, 118, 119, 135–38; Gilcrease Museum, 101–3; Oral Roberts University, 111; Philbrook Museum, 99–101
Tulsa, University of, 175, 214
Tuskahoma, Okla., 21
Two Bills Show, 119

Union Agency, 42
University of Oklahoma. See Oklahoma, University of
Urschel, Charles, 146–48

Ventura, Joe, 132
Ventura family, 132
Verdigris River, 7
Vinita, Okla., 8, 52
Voting, 76, 143–44

Wace Indians, 52
Wahkontah (Brandt), 144
Walton, Jack, 136, 137, 138
Warren, Clif, 220
Washita River, 49
Water, 189–92. See also Rivers
Watonga, Okla., 196
Watie, Stand, 47–48

Wea Indians, 52
Weatherford, Okla., 131
Welsh, xviii
Wentz, Lew, 179
Wesley, Charles, Hotel, 129–30
West Shawnee Trail, 40
West Tulsa, Okla., 135
Wewoka, Okla., 21, 87
Wheat, 94–95
White Bear, 50, 51
White horses, 33
Wichita, Kans. 40
Wichita Indians, 17, 50; language, 156
Wichita Mountains, 4
Wild West shows, 119–21
Williams (architect), xvi
Wilson, Charles Banks, 85, 160, 161, 163
Windbreaks, 189–90
Wine, 128, 141
Women, 34–35, 67–68, 90, 107, 141–43, 185 (*see also* specific persons); and drag dogs, horses, 28ff.; kitchen equipment of Indians, 22–23; Mohonk Lodge beadwork, 197–98
Woods, Silas, 72
Woolaroc Museum, 97–99
Worcester, Samuel Austin, 171
World War I veterans, 139
World War II, 107–8
WPA, 186, 189
Wright, Allan, 76
Wright, F. H., 197
Wright, Frank Lloyd, 109
Writers, 144
Wuh-tee, 151–52
Wyandot Indians, 52

Yale, Okla., 161
Yukon, Okla., xviii, 130

Ziegfeld, Florenz, 158

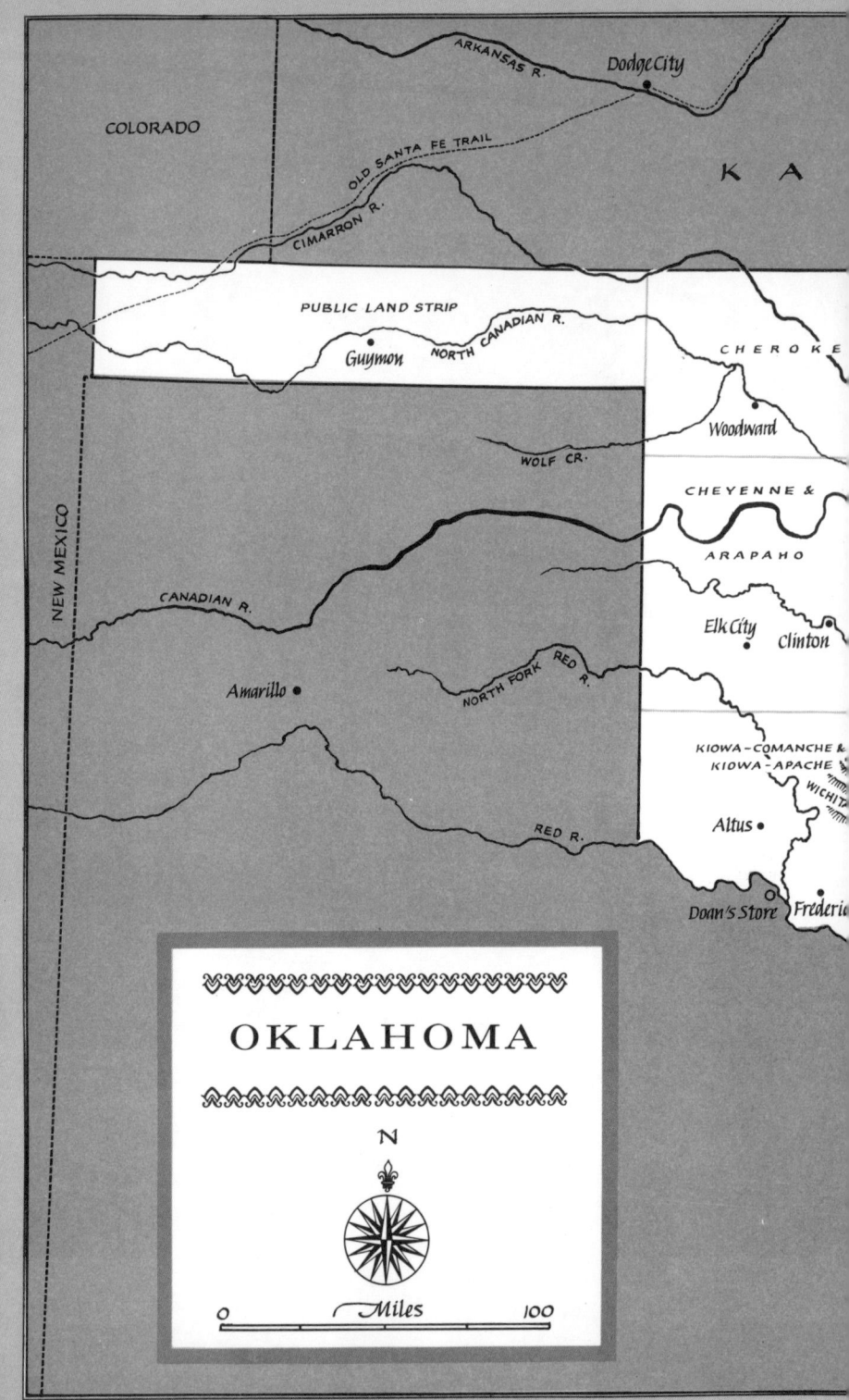